CULTURES OF THE WORLD
Austria

Cavendish
Square
New York

Published in 2017 by Cavendish Square Publishing, LLC
243 5th Avenue, Suite 136, New York, NY 10016
Copyright © 2017 by Cavendish Square Publishing, LLC

Third Edition

Library of Congress Cataloging-in-Publication Data

Names: Sheehan, Sean, 1951- author. | Nevins, Debbie, author.
Title: Austria / Sean Sheehan and Debbie Nevins.
Description: New York : Cavendish Square Publishing, 2017. | Series: Cultures of the world | Includes bibliographical references and index. | Description based on print version record and CIP data provided by publisher; resource not viewed. Identifiers: LCCN 2015045997 (print) | LCCN 2015043531 (ebook) | ISBN 9781502618429 (ebook) | ISBN 9781502618412 (library bound)
Subjects: LCSH: Austria—Juvenile literature. | Austria—History—Juvenile literature. | Austria—Social life and customs—Juvenile literature.
Classification: LCC DB17 (print) | LCC DB17 .S44 2017 (ebook) | DDC 943.6—dc23
LC record available at http://lccn.loc.gov/2015045997

Writers, Sean Sheehan; Debbie Nevins, third edition
Editorial Director, third edition: David McNamara
Editor, third edition: Debbie Nevins
Art Director, third edition: Jeffrey Talbot
Designer, third edition: Jessica Nevins
Production Manager, third edition: Jennifer Ryder-Talbot
Cover Picture Researcher: Jeffrey Talbot
Picture Researcher, third edition: Jessica Nevins

PICTURE CREDITS

PRECEDING PAGE

The Saint Sebastian church in Ramsau, Austria, is a popular subject for photographers.

Printed in the United States of America

CONTENTS

AUSTRIA TODAY

THE HILLS ARE ALIVE WITH THE SOUND OF MUSIC!"
For many people, their notion of Austria is summed up in the iconic scene of Julie Andrews singing and twirling in her *dirndl* (DURN-dahl) skirt, arms outstretched, in a meadow of wildflowers against a stunning Alpine background. The 1965 movie musical *The Sound of Music* is loosely based on the story of Maria von Trapp (1905—1987), played by Julie Andrews, a postulant (nun-in-training) at a Salzburg abbey who, in 1926, tutored one of the children of a widowed naval commander, Baron Georg von Trapp. Maria ended up marrying Georg and the family formed a singing group, the Trapp Family Singers. After the annexation of Austria by Nazi Germany in 1938, the family moved to the mountains of Stowe, Vermont, and opened an upscale, Austrian-themed resort, the Trapp Family Lodge. A Trapp grandson runs the lodge today.

The Trapp family's story, interesting as it is, was largely fictionalized in the movie, and the film contains plenty of historical inaccuracies. Nevertheless, it was a huge hit and helped form a fairytale image of Austria in the minds of millions of viewers.

The Schönbrunn Palace in Vienna served as an imperial summer residence to generations of Hapsburg emperors. Today it is the city's most popular tourist attraction.

The Republic of Austria is one of the smaller countries in the European Union (EU), occupying 32,383 square miles (83,871 square kilometers) in south-central Europe. The dramatic, snow-capped mountains of the Austrian Alps, part of a range characterized by jagged peaks and raging rivers, attract skiers from all over the continent.

Monasteries and convents from as early as the eighth century dot the landscape of this modern republic, home to eight World Heritage sites. Castles and palaces attest to Austria's imperial past, when it governed a vast and powerful empire. The scenic mountain vistas and Alpine villages are as enchanting today as in any fantasy. That's why tourism is Austria's most important economic sector. Moreover, Austria's visual beauty is not its only draw; the country's cultural heritage is as alive with the sound of music as any place could be. This, after all, is the home of Mozart.

For Austrians, however, their country is far more complex—as reality always is—than a movie set piece. Tourists who expect Austria to be *The Sound of Music* are a bit like tourists to the United States who expect to find the Wild West and all Americans to be cowboys (or some more recent Hollywood portrayal). There's a kernel of truth in these stereotypical visions, of course, but they are simplistic, outdated, and probably not all that relevant today.

In that case, what is Austria really all about? That's not an easy question to answer, for Austria is both a very old and a very new country. It has an extremely complex history; it has come and gone and come back again in various guises over the years—from powerful empire to German province to small central European country, with numerous other variations and ever-changing boundaries. It has been—or been part of—the House of Hapsburg, the Austrian Empire, the Austro-Hungarian Empire, German Austria, Nazi Germany, and finally, since 1945, a smaller, independent republic called Austria.

Austrian President Heinz Fischer attends a wreath ceremony at a Holocaust memorial on November 8, 2013, in Vienna as part of the seventy-fifth anniversary of the *Kristallnacht* pogrom.

Austrians, therefore, may have a bit of an identity problem. Their fractured history, multinational allegiances and traditions make for an uncertain heritage.

There is a darker side to Austria. For Jews during the Holocaust (1933–1945), the lovely country was a hotbed of hatred, horror, and death. For many other Austrians, it was a time they would rather forget—and they have tried. In fact, it took Austria a long time to come to terms with its past, as officials denied any responsibility for the genocide that took place there. For many years following World War II, Austria preferred to think of itself as "the first victim" of Nazi aggression. Indeed, Nazi Germany annexed Austria in 1938, and Austria essentially ceased to exist. However, when Germany first invaded Austria, there was no resistance. Recent surveys show that most Austrians continue to deny that two hundred thousand people welcomed Hitler's troops as they marched into Austria, despite overwhelming evidence that ecstatic crowds gathered at Heldenplatz in Vienna's city center to hear him deliver a rousing speech. This is not to say that all Austrians were Nazi sympathizers, of course, but there were even more Austrian members of the Nazi Party per capita than there were in Germany.

It was only in 1991 that the Austrian chancellor Franz Vranitzky officially admitted and apologized for Austria's role in the Holocaust. Since then, Austria has tried to forge a new, clear-eyed identity that admits the past but is committed to being a better country now, based on the values of freedom, democracy, and tolerance.

The European migrant crisis of 2014–2015 put that sentiment to the test. As vast numbers of refugees from the Middle East, the Balkans, and parts of Africa flooded into Europe, thousands crossed into Austria from Hungary, which had refused to accept them. At first welcoming, Austria soon found itself overwhelmed and sent the Austrian army to the Hungary border. In October 2015, Austrian authorities announced the country would build a fence along its border with Slovenia to further control the situation.

Meanwhile, the old Austrian narrow-mindedness and intolerance began to raise its head. Fair or not, Austrians have long been accused of xenophobia—

Refugees who have just crossed into Austria from Slovenia wait to board buses in October 2015 in Spielfeld, Austria.

the irrational fear and dislike of foreigners. The fact that most of the new refugees are Muslim only exacerbates that fear. In August 2015, the Austrian government explained that it is "fully committed" to the fight against racism, xenophobia, and anti-Semitism. However, the authorities also warned that "racial prejudice, attitudes and acts still exist and that sustainable policies are necessary in order to combat it long-term."

According to a report by the European Commission Against Racism and Intolerance (ECRI), the Austrian police recorded 1,900 instances of neo-Nazi activity in 2013 alone, up from 940 in the previous year and 338 in 2011. The number of racially motivated crimes has also increased, according to official statistics, increasing from 519 cases in 2012 to 574 in 2013—and that was before the migrant tide turned into a crisis. Meanwhile, Austria's conservative Freedom Party and other even farther-right parties enjoyed an electoral boost.

Austria is hardly alone in this, and tensions are natural in such an overwhelming human emergency. No one nation is going to be able to solve this or any other pan-European problem, but how Austria responds in the coming years will be a test of its commitment to its new identity. Present-day Austria is trying to recover from the damage inflicted on its international reputation by its past.

In January 2000, Chancellor Victor Klima said, "In the awareness of both historical truths—that Austrians were victims and that they were perpetrators—and in view of our responsibility for the future, there must be no doubt about the continuation of the critical confrontation with the Nazi past ... Only if we can explain to the coming generations what happened and how it could happen, can we develop in them the ability to resist any form of inhuman ideologies ... We need symbolic acts of common remembrance and collective warning never again to stray from the path of democracy and freedom."

The natural loveliness of Austria rightly deserves to be accentuated by its culture's best qualities. The foundation is there—in the elegance of Vienna, the sweetness of its pastries, the colors of its folk traditions, and of course, in the sound of music that echoes in the hearts of its people.

GEOGRAPHY

Castle ruins overlook the Danube River in the Wachau Valley near Vienna.

1

AUSTRIA IS A LANDLOCKED COUNTRY in south-central Europe. It is bordered by Germany, the Czech Republic, and Slovakia to the north; Hungary to the east; Slovenia and Italy to the south; and Switzerland and Liechtenstein to the west. Austria stretches 362 miles (583 kilometers) from east to west and 162 miles (261 km) from north to south.

Europe's Danube River passes through ten countries and four capital cities, more than any other river in the world. Austria is the second country (after Germany) and Vienna is the first capital along the Danube's course. Ten percent of the Danube River Basin's total area is in Austria.

Landlocked Austria is surrounded by many other European countries.

The snowcapped Alps in winter are a majestic sight.

Austria's main geographical feature is the Alpine mountain system crossing the country from east to west. The Alps dominate the southern and central parts of the country. Only in the north does the land flatten out into a plateau drained by the Danube River that flows eastward.

THE AUSTRIAN ALPS

The most dramatic feature of Austria's landscape, the Alps cover 64 percent of the country—from the Swiss border in the west, across the central region, and almost to the Vienna Basin in the east.

The Alps were formed some thirty million years ago when tremendous disturbances deep in the earth created pressures so strong that they caused large areas of rock to fold and rise high above the ground. At altitudes of more than 6,000 feet (1,828 m), snow is present at least half the year. On the higher peaks, the snow never melts. In the foothills and valleys of the mountains, rich pasture lands and alluvial soils have enabled farmers to make Austria almost self-sufficient in food production.

The northern Alps extend from Vorarlberg province in the west, east through central Salzburg, and to the Vienna Woods. They are the most inaccessible part of the Alps. The southern limestone Alps, which run along Austria's border with Italy and Slovenia, include the Karawanken range south of the Drava River in the province of Carinthia. In the central Alps, which contain the country's highest and most famous mountain, the Grossglockner, granite, gneiss, and schist have weathered over millions of years to form spectacular features.

CROSSING THE ALPS

Two important gaps in the mountains link Austria to neighboring countries—the Arlberg Pass in the west leading to Switzerland and the Brenner Pass going south to Italy. When it snows heavily, the Arlberg Pass may have to be

Innsbruck is the capital city of the federal state of Tyrol in western Austria.

GLACIERS

Glaciers are large masses of moving ice formed in conditions typically found in high mountain regions like the Austrian Alps. Snow collects in the folds of the mountains, and as more snow piles on, the lower layers turn into ice under the weight of the upper layers. When the ice is about 200 feet (60 meters) thick, it begins to slowly slide down the valley floor. Glaciers in the highest summits, where the temperatures at the base of the ice masses are lowest, may move as little as 3.3 feet (1 m) a year.

A glacier is like a gigantic earthmover, scraping and grooving the bedrock of the valley and making the original fold in the mountains larger and deeper. The result, a U-shaped glacial valley, is a typical feature of the Austrian landscape. Most of the country's villages and small towns are tucked into these valleys.

At the head of a glacier valley, moving ice erodes the rock and carves a deep bowl-like basin called a cirque. *Sometimes two cirques form side by side so that all that remains of the original mountain between them is a narrow ridge called an* arête. *This accounts for the slender but high mountains found in the Austrian Alps. Parallel cirques may meet at some point, crossing the arête and forming a pass called a* col.

The Pasterze Glacier, some 5 miles (8 km) long, is the longest glacier in Austria but shrinks about 33 feet (10 m) each year. It lies on Grossglockner, Austria's highest mountain.

closed, but traffic from Switzerland can continue moving into the Vorarlberg area through a tunnel under the pass. Ski resorts flourish in the Arlberg area due to the long winters.

The Brenner Pass is especially important for its low-lying position. Winter snows never block the pass, so it remains open throughout the year. The pass has been a major route for centuries for traffic moving from Italy to Germany. Today, roads and train lines continue to link the two countries.

AN ALPINE CITY

The mostly flat city of Innsbruck is nestled some 2,000 feet (600 m) above sea level on the margins of the central Alps in the valley of the green Inn River.

A 10,827-foot (3,300 m) cable-car ride starting from either the Hafelekar terminal at 7,444 feet (2,269 m) or Seegrube at 6,250 feet (1,905 m) offers a bird's eye view of the Nordkette peaks, which form a spectacular backdrop to this Alpine city. Innsbruck's landscape provides great opportunities for skiing, hiking, and cycling. Trains leaving from Innsbruck's main station, the Hauptbahnhof, pass plateau villages such as Reith and Seefeld.

The Nordkette region is breathtaking in both summer and winter.

An avalanche, or the sudden flow of snow and ice down a mountainside, is an ever-present danger in the Alps, as it is on any snow- or glacier-covered mountains. Avalanches are among the most serious of natural threats to life in mountainous terrain, particularly in regions that experience large seasonal temperature changes.

Austria regularly experiences fatalities due to these natural occurrences. In October 2015, for example, a crush of snow fell onto a road approaching the Tyrolean town of Obergugl, killing four British tourists in a car. Earlier that year, in March, a group of Australian tourists were caught in an avalanche while snowboarding in Tyrol. A young woman died in that event, and others were badly injured. In January 2015, two young Americans—Ronnie Berlack, twenty, of Franconia, New Hampshire, and Bryce Astle, nineteen, of Sandy, Utah—died in an avalanche on the Gaislachkogel, a mountain in Tyrol. They were members of the US Ski Team and were practicing for the upcoming World Cup races.

Avalanche barriers help protect ski slopes on the Kitzsteinhorn, a mountain in Austria.

One of Austria's worst avalanches, in terms of fatalities, hit the Alpine village of Galtür on February 23, 1999. The massive rush of snow buried parts of the town, killing thirty-one locals and tourists. In January 1954, an avalanche hit the Austrian village of Blons, and a second avalanche hit later that day as rescue workers were attempting to dig out the people buried by the first disaster. In all, more than two hundred people died in the double catastrophe, making for one of the worst avalanche occurrences in recorded history.

The problem with avalanches is that they cannot be predicted with much certainty. However, experts can identify conditions that are likely to cause these snowslides, and issue warnings when the danger seems high. Ski resorts and mountain towns often take preventive measures, such as erecting barriers, planting trees—which greatly reduce the strength of the snowslides—and deliberately triggering small, controllable avalanches with explosives in order to break up the structure of a threatening snowpack. Nevertheless, in Austria, about twenty-six people die each year in avalanches.

CLIMATE

Winter temperatures in Austria range from 34 to 39 degrees Fahrenheit (1 to 4 degrees Celsius), summer temperatures from 68 to 77°F (20 to 25°C). Spring and fall are usually cloudy, with temperatures between 46 and 59°F (8 and 15°C). Eastern Austria receives less than 31.5 inches (80 cm) of rain annually, the rest of the country between 28 and 79 inches (70 and 200 cm) a year.

Sheep graze in the high Alpine meadows during the short summers.

In the Alps, summers are short and winters long. The sheltered valleys facing south are filled with fog and cold air, while resorts in the mountain villages enjoy warmer and cleaner air throughout the year.

The *foehn* (sometimes spelled *föhn*) is a warm, dry southerly wind that blows down the mountains of Austria in spring and fall. The same type of wind in the Rocky Mountains and Sierra Nevadas in the United States is called the chinook. It is created when moisture condenses out of the wind onto the mountains, warming the wind as it descends the slopes. This is beneficial for farmers at high altitudes who can take advantage of the warmer climate produced.

However, the foehn also causes snow to melt and slide down the mountain slopes. Sudden rushes of snow, or avalanches, pose an immediate danger to people caught in them. Big avalanches sometimes block off roads so that small mountain communities may be cut off from the rest of the country for long periods of time.

FORESTS AND MEADOWS

Forests and woodland cover almost 40 percent of Austria. Deciduous forests of beech and oak protect mountain slopes up to about 4,000 feet (1,220 m).

High grasses poke through the waters of Lake Neusiedl.

Fir and spruce grow above 4,000 feet (1,220 m), where the soil is thinner.

Closer to the summits, coniferous forests of pine and larch dominate, but above 6,565 feet (2,001 m), trees give way to Alpine meadows. Orchids, poppies, and edelweiss grow at these heights. These flowers are unique to the Alpine landscape, having adapted to the low temperatures, strong winds, and seasonal snows. Small and compact, Alpine plants grow near the ground. They appear soon after the snow melts in the spring to make full use of the short growing season.

Lake Neusiedl in Burgenland, the largest steppe lake in Europe, is a habitat for thick reed beds covering more than half the lake's surface.

Much previously forested land around the Alps has been turned into arable land. The Danube River Valley and the eastern lowlands constitute the bulk of Austria's arable land.

FAUNA

Foxes, marten, deer, hares, badgers, squirrels, wildcats, pheasant, and partridge can be found in Austria. Chamois, ibex, and marmots inhabit the mountains. The chamois is an antelope with short horns that curve downward at the back. The ibex is a goat with large curved horns. The marmot, a rodent similar to the woodchuck, lives in a colony and hibernates. Red deer and roe deer are popular targets for hunting enthusiasts. Wolves and brown bears have completely disappeared from Austria's landscape.

Birds such as the purple heron, spoonbill, and avocet are among more than three hundred bird species in the reed beds on Lake Neusiedl. The ptarmigan, a bird that is rarely seen up close, lives in the Alps. Its feathers change color with the season: brown in summer, white in winter. In coldest weather, the ptarmigan huddles and allows itself to be buried under the snow until the weather improves.

A regular visitor to the Salzburg area is the griffon vulture from the Balkans. Even with its wingspan of 10 feet (3 m), the griffon vulture is not a common sight. Rarer yet is the golden eagle, which hunts with a partner over the same area all of its life.

Marine life in Austria includes fish such as salmon, char, pike, and catfish, amphibians such as the moor frog, and freshwater mollusks. The construction of power stations along the Austrian Danube has been a major threat to the river's marine life.

A golden eagle prepares to land on a tree stump.

THE DANUBE

The Danube River, Europe's second-largest river, flows for 1,770 miles (2,848 km) through much of central Europe. It rises in Germany and passes through ten nations before it empties into the Black Sea. Although the river's path through the provinces of Upper and Lower Austria is only 217 miles (349 km), 96 percent of the country is drained by the river and its tributaries. Where the river enters Austria from Germany the scenery is dramatic, as the valleys are narrow and either thick forests or sheer cliffs loom up on either side. In this area the river drops 3 feet (1 m) every mile (1.6 km), and the turbulent water makes it very difficult to navigate without a motorboat.

Downriver of the city of Linz, the Danube enters the Wachau Valley. Along the riverbanks, bare rocks soften into hills and dark forests yield to vineyards and orchards. Medieval castles perched on the slopes add to the romantic atmosphere. As the river approaches Vienna, it stretches out in swampy channels, but engineers have channeled the river through a canal for its passage through the city.

PROVINCES AND CITIES

Austria has nine provinces, with identities defined by topography and economy. Vienna, the federal capital, is the commercial, industrial, and administrative heart of Austria and a province in its own right. Austria's second-smallest province is Vorarlberg, at the westernmost end of the country.

Burgenland, the country's easternmost province, is predominantly agricultural, producing wheat, corn, vegetables, fruit, and wines. Lake Neusiedler, Europe's largest steppe lake, is a popular tourist attraction in Burgenland.

Carinthia, the southernmost province, has some two hundred lakes, several with popular resorts. The town of Villach near the province's borders with Slovenia and Italy, is the biggest road and rail junction in the eastern Alps. Carinthia's most important natural resources are hydroelectricity and timber.

Upper Austria is the country's second-largest source of oil and natural gas after Lower Austria. Scenic lakes in Upper Austria draw tourists to the Salzkammergut region.

Salt gave the province of Salzburg its name; salt has been mined here for centuries. Styria, on the other hand, is frequently referred to as Austria's "green province" because half of it is covered by forests and a further quarter by grassland and vineyards. Styria is also Austria's leading mining province; the Erzberg (Ore Mountain) and the town of Eisenerz (Iron Ore) are located here. Austria's automobile industry is centered in the capital of Styria, Graz.

Salzburg rises over the River Salzach.

Tyrol earns more foreign currency through tourism than does any other province of Austria. Tyrol is situated at the junction of numerous highways. Innsbruck, its capital, hosted the Winter Olympics in 1964 and 1976.

INTERNET LINKS

lawine.Tyrol.gv.at/en
The Avalanche Warning Service in Tyrol issues daily avalanche bulletins throughout the season. The site is partially in English, and the blog, which can be translated into English, includes many interesting photos and charts.

travel.nationalgeographic.com/travel/countries/austria-guide
National Geographic offers a section on Austria which includes several photo galleries.

www.tourmycountry.com/austria/geography-austria.htm
This site gives a good overview of Austria's landforms and regions.

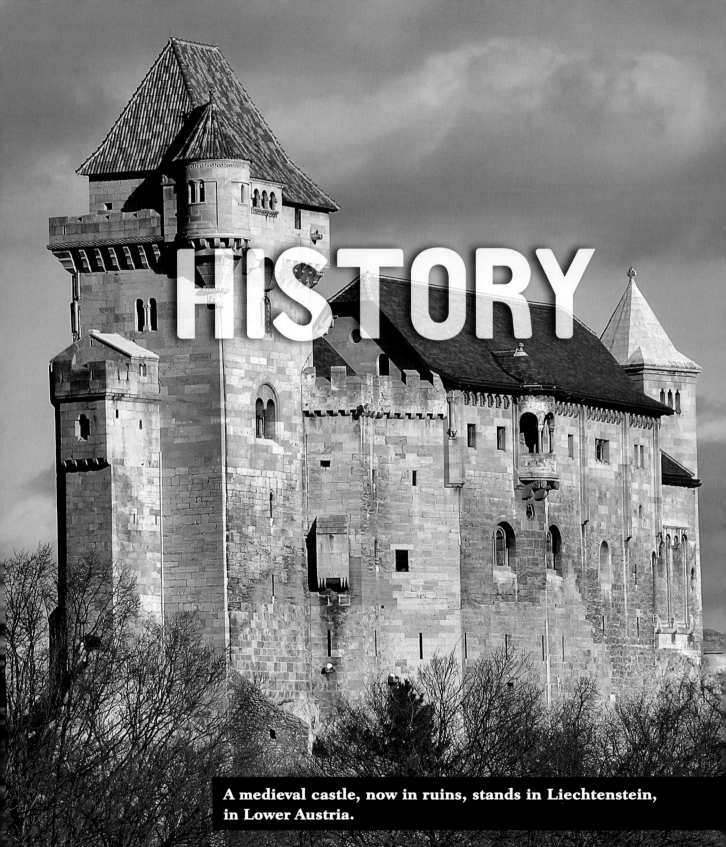

HISTORY

A medieval castle, now in ruins, stands in Liechtenstein, in Lower Austria.

2

THE STORY OF HUMAN LIFE ON THE European continent begins tens of thousands of years ago. Little is known about the hunter-gatherers who roamed the region for many millennia. In Austria, the earliest traces of human life are the remains of a Neanderthal man who lived some sixty thousand years ago. Ancient bones, stone tools, and rare stone artifacts, such as the carved female forms found in the Danube River Valley, are the only clues we have to the lives of these Stone Age people. After the last Ice Age, hunter-gatherers—and much later, farmers—settled in Austria's mountain valleys. It's likely that they traveled along the Danube.

Around 800 BCE, Austria grew into an important commercial center. Travelers followed the Danube Valley through Austria between eastern and western Europe, and the Brenner Pass was a safe route for traders going south through the Alps to Rome or Alexandria.

In the nineteenth century, the Austrian Empire was the second-largest country in Europe, after the Russian Empire, and one of the world's great powers. Its motto was *Alles Erdreich ist Österreich untertan* (All the world is subject to Austria).

In archaeology and art history, there is perhaps no artifact more intriguing than the tiny statuette called the Venus of Willendorf (VIL-en-dorf). The 4.4-inch (11.1-centimeter) sculpture was discovered in 1908 near the village of Willendorf in the Danube Valley in Lower Austria. It was carved from an oolitic limestone that is not local to the area, and was covered in a thick layer of red ochre. (Unfortunately, overzealous cleaning at the time of the discovery removed most of the red paint.)

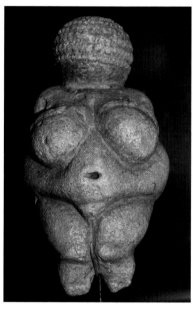

What is remarkable about the little stone woman is that she was carved around 25,000 years ago, during the Paleolithic Era, or Old Stone Age. The piece is one of the oldest known works of art. She has no face, no feet, and tiny arms. However, her hair—or perhaps it's a knit cap on her head—is carefully articulated. Her body emphasized fertility and childbearing. Both qualities would have been prized during the harsh times and the scarcity of food that these humans experienced. Researchers suggest the piece might have been a ritualistic object; but, in fact, no one knows much of anything about the Venus—who she was, who carved her, or what her purpose was.

Many academics now refer to the piece as the Woman of Willendorf, disputing the Venus terminology as culturally inaccurate; nevertheless, the piece and others like it are most well known as "Venus figurines." This term refers to a group of nude female statuettes, generally dating from 33,000 to 20,000 BCE, which have been found throughout Europe, from France to Siberia. The sculptures share the same remarkable characteristics: exaggerated torsos, obese or pregnant, and far less articulated heads and limbs. In 1988, an even older figurine was discovered in Austria, the Venus of Galgenberg (circa 30,000 BCE). Both of these important works now reside at the Naturhistorisches Museum *(Natural History Museum) in Vienna.*

How is it that prehistoric artisans living many thousands of miles and years apart created such amazingly similar figurines? That part of the Venus story remains a bewildering mystery.

From an early Celtic settlement on the banks of the Danube developed a civilization that would become a powerful European empire lasting more than six hundred years. Today, Austria's importance still derives from its unique location between the East and the West.

THE CELTS AND ROMANS

The Celts, a group of peoples inhabiting much of Europe in pre-Roman times, moved into Austria around 400 BCE, establishing the kingdom of Noricum. They stayed there for over three hundred years. They opened up copper and salt mines in Austria and established a village where Vienna is today. The Celts brought to Austria their technical skills and a love of art that is characteristic of present-day Austrians.

Around 30 BCE, Roman invaders displaced the Celts. Although the Romans had explored the Danube long before, it was not until then that they made the Danube their northern frontier against the Germanic peoples who threatened their empire.

A Roman triumphal arch, called the *Heidentor* (Pagan Gate), remains from a Roman army camp dating from the first century. It is located halfway between Vienna and Bratislava.

The Romans occupied Austria and set up the provinces of Raetia, Noricum, and Pannonia. They fortified the Celtic village on the banks of the Danube and named it Vindobona. Later, it would become Vienna.

As in other parts of Europe, the Romans built good roads and established laws that laid the foundations for the development of commerce and civic life. The Roman emperor and philosopher Marcus Aurelius spent a lot of time in Austria trying to consolidate a firm defense against the tribes of northern Europe. He died in Vindobona in 180 CE.

Roman rule in Austria lasted four centuries. Although the first two hundred years were peaceful and prosperous, later years were more turbulent.

INVASIONS AND THE HOLY ROMAN EMPIRE

The Salzburg Cathedral, a seventeenth-century Baroque church, stands today on the place where the first cathedral was built there in 774 CE.

Germanic tribes attacked Austria many times in the latter half of the second century CE. After the fifth century, when the Roman armies withdrew, Austria was occupied by Germanic tribes from the north and Slavs from the east. The Asian conqueror, Attila, and his army of Huns also raided much of the Danube Valley.

Records of these centuries are scarce and the invaders were diverse. Their legacy seems minimal compared to the impact of Christianity, which began spreading in this part of Europe around the sixth and seventh centuries as missionaries from countries like Ireland spread their beliefs and established churches. In 774 CE, a cathedral was erected in the town of Salzburg, now one of Austria's larger cities.

In 788 CE, Austria came under the control of Charlemagne, emperor of the Germanic Franks. It was Charlemagne who gave Austria its name. He called it Österreich (OOST-er-rike), meaning eastern kingdom, because it was the easternmost frontier of his empire.

Toward the end of Babenberg rule, in the late twelfth century, the Third Crusade took place. Although the Crusades were conducted as religious wars between Christian Europe and the Muslim Arabs, in reality, they were struggles for control of valuable trade routes through the Middle East. During the Third Crusade, the duke of Austria had a quarrel with the English king, Richard I, also known as Richard the Lionheart.

In 1192, when Richard was returning to England after the Crusade, he tried to pass through Austria in disguise but was discovered. The duke held him prisoner in Dürnstein Castle, overlooking the Danube. Back home in England, Richard's brother, John, ruled unjustly. This was the period of the legendary Robin Hood of Sherwood Forest, a staunch supporter of King Richard.

Legend has it that a faithful minstrel searched everywhere for the king, singing beneath every castle wall he could find. When he reached Dürnstein, Richard recognized his voice and sang along. Only after a hefty ransom was paid did the duke of Austria release the English king. Richard the Lionheart returned triumphantly to England in 1194, but he soon left for France and never returned.

Burgruine Dürnstein Castle, now a ruin, has been abandoned since 1679.

In the late ninth century, the Magyars of Hungary made continual raids into the Danube Valley and threatened to break up Charlemagne's great empire. Otto I, a German king, finally managed to defeat the Magyars at the Battle of Lech in 955 CE. Austria became an independent state, and in 962 CE, the pope crowned Otto as the Holy Roman Emperor.

THE FIRST ROYAL FAMILY

Austria's first royal family were a group of German nobles called the Babenbergs. They were originally given the land around Vienna but extended their domain to cover much of Austria. Leopold I was the first Babenberg to be appointed margrave (MAR-grave), or provincial ruler of Austria, in 976 CE by Otto II, the Holy Roman emperor. The Babenberg dynasty lasted almost three hundred years, during which Austria remained a part of the Holy Roman Empire and the Babenbergs supported the emperor in disputes with the pope. In 1156, Austria was granted the status of a duchy by the Holy Roman emperor. This was an era of prosperity; the economy grew, the Danube became an important trade route, and Vienna became established as the capital city. According to legend, Vienna flourished because of the huge ransom paid for the release of the English king, Richard the Lionheart.

Empress Maria Theresa of Austria (1717-1780)

THE HAPSBURG EMPIRE

After the last Babenberg died with no heir, Rudolf of Hapsburg became ruler of Austria. The Hapsburg dynasty ruled Austria and large areas of Europe from 1278 to 1918. The central kingdom was around Austria, Hungary, and Bohemia. Through diplomatic marriages, the Hapsburgs added territory to their empire, which eventually stretched from Spain to Hungary.

The Hapsburg Empire was so great that many wars were fought over it. In the Thirty Years War, which lasted from 1618 to 1648, Catholic Hapsburg forces fought Protestant armies from northern Europe. The greatest challenge came in the seventeenth century when the Turks almost captured Vienna, but they were pushed back and eventually defeated.

After Charles VI died in 1740, his daughter Maria Theresa became queen. Others fought her on the grounds that a woman could not become the ruler.

Some territories were lost to the Prussians in the War of Succession, but Maria Theresa proved to be one of the greatest rulers of the Hapsburg Empire. She encouraged industrial growth, lowered taxes on peasants, promoted education, and reformed the legal system.

THE EMPIRE ENDS

Austria was weakened as a result of the Napoleonic Wars at the beginning of the eighteenth century. Nevertheless, its territory still included Hungary, a part of northern Italy, and a number of German states under Austrian leadership. In 1859, however, Austria lost its Italian territories and then its leadership of the German states. In 1867, Emperor Franz Josef agreed to give greater autonomy to Hungary.

In 1908, Austria-Hungary took over some of Serbia's territory, but it was not a peaceful situation. In 1914, a Serb nationalist assassinated the heir to the Austrian throne, an event that sparked World War I. Austria-Hungary and Germany fought on one side against the allied forces of Serbia, Italy, Russia, France, and Britain.

Austria-Hungary found itself on the losing side of World War I in 1918, and its empire was divided among the victors. The last emperor abdicated, ending six hundred years of Hapsburg rule. A new Austria, one-eighth its former size, was declared a republic.

After World War I, the Austrian economy went through a difficult time. The worldwide recession in the 1930s caused mass unemployment. Many Austrians felt that their country could not survive as a separate state due to its reduced size, and there was increasing support for a union with Germany. This almost resulted in civil war. Austrian Nazis organized a coup in 1934 to overthrow the government. They assassinated Chancellor Engelbert Dollfuss but were unable to take over the government at that time. Four years later, however, the Nazis were finally victorious when Germany invaded Austria.

In 1915, during World War I, Austrian troops cling to rocks and ropes as they climb over a mountain pass to surprise Italian forces. Today this region is part of Slovenia.

AUSTRIA IN WORLD WAR II

On March 12, 1938, German troops invaded Austria and declared an *Anschluss* (ahn-SHLOOS), or forced union, with Germany. Ironically, Adolf Hitler, who was responsible for the Anschluss, was born and brought up in Austria. Hitler left Austria when he was young. In Germany, he joined and built up the Nazi Party, eventually becoming its leader. By 1934, he was the chancellor and *Führer* (leader) of Nazi Germany.

The German invasion of Austria was part of Hitler's *Heim ins Reich* (home into the empire) movement. That was a policy aimed at bringing all *Volksdeutsche* (ethnic Germans) living outside of Germany—in Poland and Austria, for example—"home" into a "Greater Germany." Although German reunification with Austria was expressly forbidden by the Treaty of Versailles, a peace agreement drawn up at the end of World War I, the invasion of Austria went largely unchallenged by the other European powers. However, a year later, after Germany invaded Poland and Hitler's empire-building ambitions became obvious, Britain declared war.

Adolf Hitler (*center*) studies maps with his generals (*right*) and the Italian dictator Benito Mussolini (*left*).

KRISTALLNACHT

Austrian Jews knew they were in danger as soon as Germany invaded Austria in March 1938. Immediately, Nazi authorities launched a brutal anti-Semitic campaign against the Jews. They instituted Germany's Nuremberg laws, which levied great restrictions against Jewish people and took away their citizenship rights. On the night of November 9–10, 1938, rampaging gangs of Nazi paramilitary forces and like-minded citizens vandalized Jewish buildings throughout Germany and Austria.

In Vienna, home to some 170,000 Jews, almost all of the city's synagogues and prayer houses were destroyed. Jews were beaten and subjected to public humiliations, such as being forced to scrub the pavements while being tormented by their fellow Austrians. The attackers broke windows in Jewish shops and stole the goods. Authorities made no move to stop the riots. The streets were littered with so much broken glass that the pogrom, or attack, became known as Kristallnacht, (Crystal Night or the Night of Broken Glass).

Broken windows were hardly the only damage. Rioters burned and ransacked thousands of Jewish-owned properties. At least twenty-seven Jews were killed, and more than six thousand were arrested and deported to concentration camps. Immediately after the pogrom, Jewish children were banned from public schools. Kristallnacht has come to be regarded as the opening salvo of the Holocaust.

Members of the *Hitlerjugend* (Hitler Youth) force Jews to clean a street by hand as a crowd looks on in Vienna, 1938.

Kurt Waldheim (1918–2007) was one of Austria's most important international figures of the twentieth century. He served as secretary-general of the United Nations (UN) from 1971 to 1981, and then went on to become president of Austria from 1986 to 1992.

His term as president was marred by allegations that he had participated in Nazi atrocities during World War II. During the war, he had served as an intelligence officer in the Wehrmacht, *the armed forces of Nazi Germany. Waldheim denied these allegations, but even after his election as president, the allegations persisted. Historians uncovered evidence linking him to war crimes in the Balkans— his signature appeared on documents relating to the massacres and deportations of thousands of Jews.*

"Kurt Waldheim did not, in fact, order, incite or personally commit what is commonly called a war crime," wrote US historian Robert Edwin Herzstein. "But this nonguilt must not be confused with innocence. The fact that Waldheim played a significant role in military units that unquestionably committed war crimes makes him at the very least morally complicit in those crimes."

As president, Waldheim faced international isolation. In 1988, the United States put Waldheim on its list of undesirable aliens and forbid him to enter the country. A commission of international historians investigated the allegations and found that while there was no proof of Waldheim's direct personal guilt, he had to have known—despite his denials—about the Nazi war crimes that he was enabling. Waldheim refused to fully explain himself or express misgivings about his wartime role, saying, "I did my duty like hundreds of thousands of Austrians."

Waldheim did not seek re-election. He lived out the remainder of his life quietly, insisting to the end that he was just an ordinary Austrian caught up in extraordinary circumstances. He left behind a mixed legacy, praised by some for his efforts to win peace throughout the world (in his role as UN secretary-general), and criticized by many for his refusal to accept responsibility for his past.

With the Anschluss, the German-speaking Republic of Austria ceased to exist as an independent state. The Nazis began a process of extermination of people deemed to be inferior and unwanted. They established death camps in Poland. In what came to be called the Holocaust, thousands of Austrian Jews were sent to their deaths in gas chambers in these camps. In Austria, the Nazis built a concentration camp near the village of Mauthausen on the Danube; thousands of people were murdered there. The infamous Adolf Eichmann, one of the architects of the Holocaust, was Austrian. So, too, was Amon Goeth, commandant of the Plaszow concentration camp in Poland.

AFTER THE WAR

World War II ended in Austria when Allied troops captured it in March 1945. The Allies—the United States, Britain, France, and the Soviet Union—occupied the country, elections were held, and a provisional government took over. Austria was no longer part of Germany, but it wasn't fully independent until ten years later when Allied forces finally withdrew from the country.

Allied commanders march through the streets of Vienna during the Allied occupation at the end of World War II.

The flags of Austria and the European Union fly side by side.

Eager to ensure future peace, the Austrian parliament immediately declared the nation's permanent neutrality. Over the years, however, Austria has redefined that concept, and has forged certain alliances with Europe—it joined the European Union in 1995. It has not joined the North Atlantic Treaty Organization (NATO), the mutual defense organization of North American and European nations, but participates in peacekeeping assignments as part of NATO's Partnership for Peace. Some Austrians want to see an even stronger integration with Europe.

REFUGEES AND XENOPHOBIA

Over the years, Austrians have gained a certain reputation for xenophobia. However, it is mostly a stereotype. Since 1997, Austria has been part of the Schengen Area of the Europe Union, a group of twenty-six European nations that have opened their borders to fellow members.

In the late 1980s, the collapse of communism in the Soviet Union had a major impact on Austria. Many countries in Eastern Europe rejected communism. As East Germany knocked down the Berlin Wall, other Eastern bloc countries gradually overthrew their communist leaders as well. A wave of revolutions led to the collapse of the Soviet system.

This led to mass emigration of Eastern Europeans in search of a new life in the West. The influx of immigrants to Austria raised tensions among a section of the population, and the ultraconservative, anti-immigration Freedom Party (FPÖ) under the leadership of Jörg Haider grew in popularity, leading to fears of a revival of Nazism in Austria. Indeed, despite the country's anti-Nazi laws, Neo-Nazi groups continue to operate secretly.

The influx of refugees from the former Yugoslavia in the 1990s further fueled a fear of foreigners that prevailed among some Austrians. Haider and his party were able to exploit this fear and greatly influence the 1999 elections. (Haider—who left the Freedom Party in 2005 to form a somewhat more moderate political party, the Alliance for Austria's Future—was killed in a car crash in 2008.)

More recently, in 2015, refugees again became a major concern. Millions of asylum seekers flooded into Europe from violence in Middle Eastern countries—particularly Syria—as well as from Africa and South Asia. The migrant crisis triggered the rise of anti-immigrant (particularly anti-Muslim) feelings among some Austrians, encouraged by the political rhetoric of the FPÖ and other right-wing factions.

Protesters carry a banner reading "We are afraid" during an anti-immigrants rally in Spielfeld, Austria, near the Austria-Slovenia border on October 31, 2015.

INTERNET LINKS

www.historyplace.com/worldwar2/triumph/tr-austria.htm
"Nazis Take Austria" is a lively essay on Hitler's invasion of Austria in 1938.

www.khanacademy.org/humanities/prehistoric-art/paleolithic-art/v/nude-woman-venus-of-willendorf-c-28-000-25-000-b-c-e
"Nude woman (Venus of Willendorf)" is an excellent video presented by Khan Academy.

www.lonelyplanet.com/austria/history#146103
Lonely Planet offers a very good overview of Austria's history.

www.nytimes.com/2007/06/14/world/europe/14iht-waldheim.3.6141106.html
The *New York Times* obituary for Kurt Waldheim reviews his life, accomplishments, and secrets.

GOVERNMENT

The statue of Pallas Athena, the Greek goddess of wisdom, towers above a fountain at the entrance to the Austrian parliament building.

3

AFTER THE WITHDRAWAL OF foreign troops in 1955, Austria began to rebuild its identity as an independent country with a new spirit of cooperation, determined to avoid the conflicts of the past. Austria today is a federal republic, a union of states with a democratic form of government based on a constitution. It is made up of nine provinces, each of which has a governor and a legislature with elected officials that can pass laws relating to the province.

Austria's government structure, therefore, is similar to that of much larger federal republics, such as the United States. It has a bicameral, or two-house, parliament and a separation of powers. Austria's small size (slightly smaller than the state of Maine) makes it impractical for its states to have much autonomy, however, and most matters of importance lie within the jurisdiction of the federal government. This is also true for the judiciary system, which is exclusively federal in Austria, meaning there are no state courts.

THE CONSTITUTION

Austria has had many constitutions over the centuries, but the one in use today dates to the 1920s, which was drafted following the collapse of Austria-Hungary after World War I. It has since been modified a number of times. Its core is the *Bundes-Verfassungsgesetz* (Federal Constitutional Law), or B-VG. Although there is no bill of rights, provisions on civil liberties are split up over various constitutional legislative acts within the document.

During the years that Austria was incorporated into Germany, from 1938 to 1945, the B-VG was void and superceded by the Weimar Constitution of the German Reich, which the Nazis had already greatly modified to their own purposes. After World War II, when Austria regained its independence, its constitution was reinstated, with the important amendment establishing permanent neutrality:

1) For the purpose of the permanent maintenance of her external independence and for the purpose of the inviolability of her territory, Austria of her own free will declares herewith her permanent neutrality which she is resolved to maintain and defend with all the means at her disposal.

2) In order to secure these purposes Austria will never in the future accede to any military alliances nor permit the establishment of military bases of foreign States on her territory.

Unlike many other constitutions, the Austrian document does not begin with a preamble, or introduction. Typically, constitutional preambles state the purposes and guiding moral principles of the document, as well as providing the source of the government's authority. Austria Federal Constitutional Law begins with Act 1, which is, simply, "Austria is a democratic republic. Its law emanates from the people."

THE RIGHT TO VOTE

The right to change their government peacefully is a freedom guaranteed to Austrian citizens by the constitution, and Austrians exercise this right by voting in periodic, free, and fair elections. Austrians also have the right to vote in or to be a candidate in elections to the European Parliament,

the parliamentary institution of the European Union. The 751 European Parliament members are elected every five years by direct universal voting through proportional representation. Austrian representatives make up 2.4 percent of the total, which in 2014 was eighteen Members of the European Parliament (MEPs).

While Austrian voters generally abide by their country's own rules during elections to the European Parliament, they share some rules with the citizens of other EU nations, such as the right to vote from eighteen years of age, equality for men and women, and ballot secrecy.

THE FEDERAL GOVERNMENT

The government of the Republic of Austria has an executive branch, a legislative branch called the Federal Assembly, and a judicial branch headed by the Supreme Judicial Court.

THE EXECUTIVE BRANCH The executive branch is headed by a president and chancellor. The chancellor is like a prime minister. He is the head of

Members of Parliament meet in Vienna on September 1, 2015, to discuss the fair distribution of asylum seekers among the Austrian states.

Austrian Federal Chancellor Werner Faymann in 2015.

the government. The chancellor is the leader of the political party holding the majority of seats in the legislature. He is backed by a cabinet of ministers, whom he chooses.

The federal president is the head of state. He or she is elected by all citizens for a term of six years. The president appoints the chancellor and is the commander-in-chief of the armed forces. In reality, the president is more of a figurehead and usually follows the suggestions of the chancellor in making important decisions.

THE FEDERAL ASSEMBLY The bicameral Federal Assembly consists of a National Council and a Federal Council. The Federal Council consists of sixty-two representatives from the nine provinces. Each province elects its representatives as well as successors should the representatives be unable to complete their terms. The usual term is six years.

The federal president decides the number of representatives each province is entitled to, based on the last census. The maximum number of representatives a province may have in the Federal Council is twelve; the minimum is three.

The 183-member National Council represents the country as a whole. The National Council is the more important arm of the legislative body. While bills apart from the budget need approval from both the Federal Council and the National Council, the National Council can override a Federal Council veto by a simple majority vote. Members serve five-year terms.

THE JUDICIAL BRANCH The highest courts include the *Oberster Gerichtshof* ("Supreme Court of Justice"), the *Verfassungsgerichtshof* ("Constitutional Court"), and the *Verwaltungsgerichtshof* ("Administrative Court"). The Supreme Court of Justice consists of eighty-five judges; the

Constitutional Court consists of twenty judges. Both the Supreme and Constitutional court judges are nominated by executive branch departments and appointed by the president. These judges serve for life. The two administrative judges are recommended by executive branch departments and are appointed by the president for terms determined by the president. Austria's 134 district and 18 regional courts are also administered by the federal government.

The mayor of Vienna, Michael Häupl (*left*), of the Social Democrats shares a smile with his challenger, Heinz-Christian Strache, the head of Austria's far-right Freedom Party, after elections in Vienna in October 2015.

POLITICAL PARTIES

Austria has a multi-party system, with more than seven hundred registered political parties. However, since the 1980s, only a few parties have consistently received enough votes to attain seats in the national parliament: the Social Democratic Party (SPÖ), the conservative Austrian People's Party (ÖVP), and the right-wing Freedom Party (FPÖ). Other parties that occasionally have representation in federal or state parliaments include the Greens, the Communists, the Alliance for the Future of Austria, and a right-wing populist party called Team Stronach.

Until the late 1990s, elections followed a fairly predictable pattern. For many years Austrians tended to vote for one or the other of two parties. People in the cities preferred the Social Democratic Party, which had ties to the trade unions, while people in the countryside tended to vote for the People's Party, a more conservative party with links to the Catholic Church.

On average, each party had an almost equal share of votes, making it

The Freedom Party's ideology is anti-immigrant, anti-European Union, and pro-Austrian nationalism. It campaigned in the 1999 elections with slogans like "Stop der berfremdung. Österreich zuerst." ("Stop the foreign tide. Put Austria first.") Jörg Haider's party took a surprising second place in the elections with 26.9 percent of the vote, gaining more than fifty seats in the parliament.

In 2000, the Social Democratic Party and the People's Party formed a new coalition government that included the Freedom Party, despite the objections of some European Union countries. Soon after the formation of the new coalition, Haider resigned as the leader of his party and did not take any post in the new administration. However, there was widespread belief that Haider's resignation was only a way of deflecting international criticism. Many Austrians, feeling that their country was being unfairly portrayed as a supporter of neo-Nazi policies, organized a public campaign called Widerstand *(Vee-der-stand), or "Resistance." They wanted to show the world that liberalism and tolerance were still core values in Austrian society. The Freedom Party's political gains fell in subsequent elections.*

Since 2005, the party has been headed by Heinz-Christian Strache, and in recent years it has once again gained popularity, particularly among people under the age of thirty. An increasing tide of refugees from the Middle East has only inflamed the party's nationalistic rhetoric against Muslims and immigrants. In 2015, the Freedom Party made substantial gains in local elections, no doubt fueled by Europe's migrant crisis.

difficult for either to form a majority government that could rule effectively on its own. In practice, the two parties formed a coalition and shared the important posts.

While coalition governments in some countries tend not to survive long, with political rivalries becoming bitter and persistent, the system in Austria worked surprisingly well and the citizens were generally content with their coalition government.

The 1999 general elections, however, changed political life in Austria in a very dramatic way (although it did not bring the system of coalition governments to an end). For the first time since the 1950s, a third party—the Freedom Party—gained enough votes to upset the usual result of general elections and make Austrian politics the talk of newspapers all over Europe.

Heinz-Christian Strache, the head of Austria's far-right Freedom Party, addresses journalists following local elections in 2015.

INTERNET LINKS

www.bka.gv.at/site/3327/Default.aspx
This is the home site of the Austrian Federal Government, in English.

www.cia.gov/library/publications/the-world-factbook/geos/au.html
The World Factbook has up-to-date information on the structure and leadership of Austria's government and political parties.

www.nationsonline.org/oneworld/austria.htm
This page provides links to many official Austrian sites.

ECONOMY

A woman exchanges Austrian schillings for euros at an Austrian bank in 2012.

4

USTRIA IS A WEALTHY COUNTRY with a skilled and educated labor force. Austrians enjoy a high standard of living and the economy is basically healthy. Among European countries, Austria has one of the lowest unemployment rates, at 5.6 percent, though it has been growing in recent years. In 2013, 2014, and 2015, however, economic growth was quite sluggish, which sounded alarm bells throughout Austria's—and the EU's—economic community.

Around twenty thousand organic farmers manage almost 16 percent of Austria's agricultural land. Around 10 percent of their organic production is exported. The most important product groups are dairy products, fresh fruit and vegetables, meat and meat products.

ECONOMIC CHANGES

Since 1995 Austria has been a member of the European Union. In 2002 Austria adopted the common European currency, the euro. Austria's old currency, the Schilling, is no longer accepted as legal tender. The advantage of sharing the same currency with other EU nations that have adopted the euro is that citizens of these countries can complete transactions without having to make currency exchanges. This simplifies economic life for both individuals and companies.

The Austrian economy is based mostly on private ownership, with the government operating several major companies. Government ownership of important industries goes back to the post—World War II period when government investment became necessary to rebuild a war-devastated economy. Thus the coal and oil industries, iron and steel production, and electricity generation came under government control. Now privatization is gradually reducing the government's role.

The service sector makes up the largest part, by far, of Austria's economy. It employs 68.4 percent of the country's workers and generates 70.2 percent of economic production (as measured by gross domestic product, or GDP). In Vienna, finance and law are the leading service corporations, and nationwide, tourism plays a major role.

INDUSTRY

Austria's industrial sector revolves around the use of the country's natural resources. The larger industrial works are spread across the country, with the heaviest concentration of factories in the vicinity of Vienna, where approximately 20 percent of the national population live and work.

The industrial area of Linz, Austria's third-largest city, is lit up at night.

Other manufacturing areas are found near large towns like Graz, the second-largest city in Austria. In Styria, important supplies of iron ore provide the basis for the steel industry. Austria also produces graphite, zinc, salt, lead, and copper, among other minerals.

After World War II, extensive programs were implemented to develop heavy industries, such as hydroelectric power generation, oil, natural gas, chemicals, mining, and textiles. While these programs have helped to bolster a prosperous and fairly stable economy, they have also resulted in a change in the country's character and traditions. More and more Austrians, especially the younger generation, now leave the countryside for the cities in search of employment.

In Vienna, factories producing cars, locomotives, and other vehicles employ a large number of people. Other major sources of employment are food-processing factories, textile and clothing factories, and plants that manufacture furniture, paper and pulp, optical instruments, and porcelain and glass products.

The OMV refinery in Schwechat, outside Vienna. OMV is the Austrian national oil company.

In this aerial view, the agricultural fields of Austria look like a patchwork quilt.

Austria prides itself on manufacturing quality rather than mere quantity. Many of the country's factories count the number of their employees in the hundreds rather than in the thousands. Products that Austria is famous for, such as quality glassware, porcelain, and jewelry, require the input of highly skilled craftspeople more than that of assembly-line workers.

FORESTRY AND AGRICULTURE

Much of Austria's cultivated land is used for forestry. Spruce and other conifers are planted, left to mature, and then cut down for commercial use. Reforestation is ongoing, so there is little of the original forest that once carpeted much of central Europe. A lot of timber is exported untreated. Timber processed within the country is turned into paper for export.

Most farms in Austria are family-run and usually smaller than 52 acres (21 hectares). Like most farms in Western Europe, they are small and fragmented, especially in mountainous areas. Nevertheless, the agricultural sector is highly developed. For example, on many farms, modern tractors are equipped with satellite-controlled navigation and mapping systems that help the farmer achieve targeted yields.

For many, agriculture is a part-time concern; tourism provides their primary source of income. Farmers rent out rooms or work as mountain guides or ski instructors in popular tourist areas like Tyrol. In regions bordering the Czech Republic, Slovakia, Hungary, and Slovenia, there is little tourism and the farming population is dwindling.

Since mountain slopes are not friendly to modern machinery and tourism offers farmers better financial benefits, the government gives out subsidies to mountain farmers in an effort to preserve mountain farming and the cultural landscape in the Alps.

Although less than 20 percent of Austria's land is suitable for growing crops, and only 5.5 percent of the country's labor force works in agriculture, 80 percent of its food supply comes from its farms. Among the crops grown are potatoes, wheat, barley, corn, sugar beets,

A cow enjoys the summer weather in the Alps.

rye, oats, and fruit such as grapes for wine. Since grass and clover grow well, most Alpine farmers also rear cattle. There are even pipelines to transport milk from highland farms to points in the valleys below.

Austria has a reputation for brewing high-quality lager. There are small breweries that dominate their local areas and also large national companies that produce specialty beers such as *Weissbier* (VISE-beer), a fizzy wheat beer. Austrian white wine is world famous. Burgenland produces most of Austria's red wine.

The Alpine village of Hallstatt, on the Hallstätter See, a spectacular mountain lake, is possibly Austria's most photographed village.

TOURISM

Tourism is vitally important to the Austrian economy and is its fastest-growing sector. In 2014, more than 37.6 million tourists visited Austria, which set a record for the country. Most visitors to Austria come from Western Europe, mainly Germany (perhaps attracted by the common language), followed by the Netherlands, Switzerland, Italy, and Great Britain. Recently, the winter ski resorts have begun to attract more Eastern Europeans, Russians, and Americans.

Tourism accounts for some 15 percent of Austria's economy (as measured by GDP). The mountain resorts draw visitors all year round. The top three cities tourists visit are: Vienna, the country's capital; Salzburg, with its world-famous music festivals and romantic architecture; and Innsbruck, beautifully situated amid mountains.

For scenic beauty, popular tourist destinations are the provinces of Tyrol, Salzburg, Carinthia, and Vienna, and the country's lake district, Salzkammergut, southeast of Salzburg.

The effect of tourism can be seen in the way new houses are built in the western provinces. An extra floor is added for the purpose of renting rooms to visitors. The price to pay for such large-scale tourism is the change in the social structure of valley life in these regions. Some people feel that customs and traditions are trivialized and their cultural meaning lost when they are commercialized for the tourism industry.

Tourists flock to the Graben, Vienna's most famous area for shopping.

INTERNET LINKS

www.advantageaustria.org
This Austrian business site has sections on various aspects of Austria's economy.

www.austria.info/us/basic-facts/about-austria/trade-industry
Austria, the official travel guide site, has a small section on trade and industry.

www.austria.org/economy
The Austrian Embassy in Washington, DC, offers a quick overview of the country's economy.

ENVIRONMENT

A skier in the Austrian Alps takes in the view from a snowy mountaintop.

5

AUSTRIANS TAKE AN ACTIVE INTEREST in their natural environment. After World War II, the country's first priorities were rebuilding as an independent industrial nation. Rapid economic development in the 1960s triggered a rise in industrial pollution, acid rain, and energy use, and by the 1970s, people began paying attention to environmental issues. Concerned Austrians formed a new Grüne (Green) political party, government officials passed new laws, and the people set out to preserve the natural health and beauty of their country.

Recognizing that environmental protection is a global challenge, Austria has joined in international efforts to effectively address urgent issues such as global warming. For example, Austria is part of the International Commission for the Protection of the Alps (CIPRA), an organization that seeks to preserve the natural and cultural heritage of the Alps.

More than 96 percent of Austria drains to the Danube River and accounts for about 10 percent of the entire Danube River Basin. More than 40 percent of Austria's Danube Basin is used for agriculture, settlements, and infrastructure. The rest is predominantly mountainous and generally not well suited to such usage.

CONSERVATION

Forests are important in helping to prevent avalanches, floods, and soil erosion. The Austrian government is aware that large-scale replanting programs are necessary if the country's forests are to be preserved. Austria practices reforestation for trees with commercial uses. Replanted spruce and fir, for example, are harvested for the production of paper as well as to supply lumber to the construction industry. Forest conservation laws are also in place. Austria's Forestry Act, instituted more than thirty-five years ago, created rules for planting new trees whenever existing ones are cut down.

The Alpine meadows are home to a colorful variety of flowers found nowhere else. The small white edelweiss, a typical Alpine flower made famous by the film *The Sound of Music*, is a highly protected flower; it is strictly against the law to pick it.

There are also laws for the protection of endangered animals. The chamois, for example, could disappear completely from the Austrian landscape unless given rigorous protection. The Danube, once brimming

Harvested logs sit on a forest roadside in Tyrol.

with more than seventy species of fish, is losing its diversity of marine life due to pollution. It is possible that the giant catfish, for instance, which is capable of growing up to 13 feet (4 m) long, will one day cease to swim Austria's waters.

WILDLIFE PROTECTION

Austria has the largest primeval riverine forest in Europe—the Hainburg Forest north of Burgenland at 31 square miles (80 sq km). For almost a decade, a pristine stretch of the Danube River there lay under threat as proposals were made to build a large hydroelectric plant, raising concern that it would destroy as much as 10 percent of the forest and prevent the annual spring flooding of the rest of the forest. Supporters of the project argued that the plant would mean fewer fossil-fueled power stations and less acid rain. Critics pointed out that if the Danube ceased to flow through and be cleansed by the forest, the groundwater that Vienna depended on would become polluted.

In 1996, 38.6 square miles (100 sq km) of the forest were officially declared the *Donauauen* (Danube Flood Plain) National Park. Today the park is home to approximately seven hundred species of plants, thirty species of mammals, one hundred species of birds that breed in this area, eight species of reptiles, thirteen species of amphibians, and sixty species of fish.

The wels catfish is the largest freshwater fish in Europe.

NATIONAL PARKS

Austria has six national parks, sixty nature preserves, and twenty Alpine gardens. About one-third of Austria's forested land—around 4,315 square miles (11,177 sq km)—has been officially declared as protected. Some fifty ancient woodland areas have been designated as natural reserves protected by law.

Austria's first national park, Hohe Tauern, was established in 1981. Covering approximately 695 square miles (1,800 sq km) in western Austria,

Two mountaineers climb to the summit of Grossglockner.

the park straddles the provinces of Carinthia, Salzburg, and Tyrol, and includes Austria's highest mountain, Grossglockner. In 2001, the International Union for Conservation of Nature (IUCN) granted Hohe Tauern international status as a national park.

Other national parks in Austria include the Neusiedlersee—Seewinkel, on the Hungarian border, which is a habitat for some 340 species of birds. The Thayatal National Park, on the border of the Czech Republic, features exceptional biodiversity in the beautiful Thaya River Valley landscape of steep cliffs and dense forest. It is home to the rare black stork, as well as more than one hundred other bird species.

ENERGY

Most of Austria's energy, between 60 and 70 percent, comes from hydroelectric power. Approximately 150 large and 3,000 small hydro power facilities generate electricity. In a country with Austria's hilly topography, wind power is also an advantageous source of power. In 2008, Austria was the world's seventeenth-largest producer of wind power. Nevertheless, wind power plays a small role in the country's overall energy scene. In 2013, the contribution of wind power, solar thermal power, and all other alternative sources together was only 8.1 percent of the total. The rest of the country's energy needs come from fossil fuel sources such as oil, natural gas, and coal.

Wind turbines spin in vineyards in eastern Austria.

NUCLEAR POWER In 1986, Austria experienced severe contamination by radioactive fallout following the Chernobyl nuclear disaster in the former Soviet Union. Thousands of tons of food had to be destroyed. The disaster also settled controversy over the future of Austria's Zwentendorf nuclear plant. This plant had been completed in 1978 but was never opened because of opposition within Austria to nuclear power. After the Chernobyl disaster, the plant was dismantled piece by piece and sold to anyone who wanted spare parts for a nuclear power station. In 1997, the Austrian parliament unanimously passed legislation to remain an anti-nuclear country.

AUSTRIAN ENERGY STRATEGY 2020 Austria's membership in the European Union adds specific energy requirements to the country's own policies. To achieve those goals, Austria has developed the Austrian Energy Strategy. According to the EU energy and climate package adopted in December 2008, Austria is obligated through 2020 to carry out a special energy strategy with which to achieve:
- an increase in the share of renewable energy to 34 percent,
- a reduction of the greenhouse gas emissions in sectors not subject to emissions trading by at least 16 percent, and
- a 20 percent growth in energy efficiency.

THE IMPACT OF GLOBAL WARMING

In the Alps, the average temperature has risen almost twice as fast as the global average over the last 150 years. Researchers are predicting a further 3.6°F (2°C) increase over the next forty years. That might not seem like much, but it's enough to effect widespread change, especially in the Alps. Global warming is melting Alpine glaciers. In recent decades many Alpine glaciers have shrunk to half their earlier size, and by the end of the century, all the glaciers of the Alps, with a few exceptions, will probably have melted away. As the glaciers recede, there is an increase of rock falls, landslides, and mudslides.

Wooden chalets in the Austrian Alps make for a scenic view.

Naturally, this is hurting European winter tourism. The economic consequences are nowhere more alarming than in Austria, where most of the country's skiing activity takes place at altitudes of less than 3,281 feet (1,000 m) above sea level. Snow at these heights is especially susceptible to temperature increases. As the Alps warm up and snow lines recede (possibly by as much as 1,968 feet, or 600 meters, within fifteen years), many low-level resorts in Austria may in the future receive no snow and have to shut down. The consequences of this global environmental problem for the Austrian economy will be dramatic as skiers spend their winter vacations elsewhere, jobs are lost, and national income decreases. No other country is as dependent on skiing.

The intensity and timing of Alpine snowfall are changing, resulting in short heavy falls and causing avalanches among other problems. Scientists have found with satellite imaging that the Po Valley and the region around the Alps in Austria, Germany, and Switzerland are receiving less snow cover than in the past. At Austria's lower-altitude resorts, warmer days at the beginning and end of winter mean shorter ski seasons that cut Christmas and Easter tourist traffic.

ALPINE TRAFFIC JAMS

Increased traffic not only causes annoyance for drivers but an increase in air pollution. The traffic of the Brenner Mountain Pass, for example, a major north-south transit route through the Alps on the border between Austria and Italy, rocketed from six hundred thousand vehicles per year in the early 1970s to some ten million vehicles per year only twenty years later. Since then, traffic has increased even more. More than a million trucks lumber across the Brenner Pass every year, emitting soot particles into the air.

Activists in Tyrol have held protests at the Brenner Pass against truck traffic over the Alps. There have also been demands to increase rail transportation in preference to freight trucks. The government has responded by limiting the size of international trucks crossing the country, especially via the Brenner Pass, and by looking to the rail system as a cleaner alternative for moving freight. In 2011, work began on a series of tunnels under the pass intended to increase rail traffic load. Funding issues, however, have delayed the estimated date of the tunnels' completion, pushing it back (so far) to 2025.

INTERNET LINKS

www.austria.info/us/activities/walking-hiking/national-parks-in-austria
This site has information about Austria's national parks.

www.bmlfuw.gv.at/en.html
The Austrian Federal Ministry of Agriculture, Forestry, Environment and Water Management covers a wide selection of topics in English.

www.cipra.org/en
This environmental organization works to protect the Alps.

AUSTRIANS

An Austrian woman wears a traditional dirndl outfit.

WHO IS AN AUSTRIAN? THE answer could be tricky. In recent centuries, the country itself has come and gone, grown and shrunk. Austria has been merged with Hungary (1867—1918) and Germany (1938—1945). Historically, Austrians were considered Germans and thought of themselves as such—after all, they did speak German—but those days are gone.

Twin brothers are ready for winter fun.

6

The people of South Tyrol are Italian citizens but are Austrians at heart. Italy's northernmost province, which also bears the Italian name Alto Adige, borders on the Austrian state of Tyrol, and at least 64 percent of its population speaks German. Historically a part of Tyrol, the province was split after World War I and given to Italy. A century later, many citizens still identify as Austrian.

Today's Austrians are proud of their independent identity and are acutely conscious of not being German. Nevertheless, Austrians are not simply one people. A Viennese will say that he or she is as different from someone who lives in Vorarlberg as cheese is from stone, and the person from Vorarlberg will readily agree. Yet both will emphatically assert that they are Austrians.

REGIONAL DIFFERENCES

Austria is a federation of nine provinces, many of which have their own distinct character. People from Vienna are different in some ways than people from Tyrol or Salzburg or Carinthia or Burgenland. Identifying someone simply as Austrian ignores their unique regional traits.

The most important factor accounting for these variations is Austria's landlocked location and its proximity to so many other countries. This has in the past led to population shifts and cultural "invasions," the legacies of which significantly determine the traits that distinguish one part of Austria from another today.

Austria's geography also influenced its cultural development. The physical barriers created by the Alps nurtured cultural differences across regions and even across small communities. Austrians from one valley settlement, for example, may dress differently and speak a different dialect from Austrians in another town or village a few miles away.

BURGENLANDERS

Burgenland is the least visited region of Austria. Its capital is Eisenstadt. Being close to Hungary has meant that the people of Burgenland, or Burgenlanders, have been exposed to Hungarian culture more than people in any other part of Austria have been.

Burgenland is one of only two regions in Austria where German is not the common language. An important Croatian minority lives among the three hundred thousand Burgenlanders, and Croat is the preferred language.

Historically, Burgenlanders have closer links with Hungary than with Austria. In the breakup of the Austro-Hungarian Empire after World War I,

a plebiscite to decide between autonomy or affiliation resulted in a slice of Hungary (now Burgenland) becoming a part of Austria.

Burgenland does not look typically Austrian. There are no snowy mountains, and the people are mostly fruit and vegetable farmers. Their produce is seasonal, reaping profits in the spring and summer but not during the winter. Without tourism to supplement their living, many Burgenlanders head for other parts of the country. There are significant numbers of Burgenland construction workers employed in Vienna.

STYRIANS

Some 1.2 million people live in Styria. Their capital, Graz, is Austria's largest city after Vienna. Living near Slovenia, Hungary, and Italy might explain Styrians' strong sense of independence. A writer once recounted how at a farmhouse near Graz, he found out that the lamb and wine he was having for dinner were both local produce. He asked the farmer why such

Fields green up in spring in Burgenland.

ICEMAN OF THE ALPS

In 1991, two German tourists hiking in the Ötztal Alps in Tyrol discovered the body of a man frozen in a glacier on the Austrian-Italian border. Usually, a frozen body emerging from the snow and ice in this region is that of a recent avalanche victim or mountaineer. In fact, that's what the hikers first thought. But this body was different in more ways than one.

The man lying under the ice was clutching an axe and beside him lay a knife, a flint, and a quiver of arrows. While some scientists speculated that the body could have been up to five hundred years old, glacier specialists said it was unlikely for a glacier to be able to preserve a body that long. So well-preserved was this particular discovery that it still had skin and muscle tissue. The skeleton was complete and the head and back showed signs of violent injuries.

At the University of Innsbruck, experts finally determined the body to be 5,300 years old. Ötzi, as he came to be called, is the best-preserved Stone Age man in the world. How had he been preserved so long in ice? One theory is that he had been mummified by freezing air before he fell into the glacier. The "Iceman" was about forty-five years old, stood about 5 feet, 5 inches (1.6 m) tall, and, when he was alive, weighed about 110 pounds (50 kilograms). His clothes were made from animal skins and tree bark. Near him were found chamois hairs, pieces of birchbark sewn together, a wooden backpack, a stone necklace, and a leather pouch.

Researchers found the remains of his last several meals in his stomach and intestines. He had eaten ibex, chamois, and red deer meat, along with herb bread, grains, roots, and fruits. Scientists have been able to determine an amazing amount of information about the man and his life, but one thing no one knows: Why did he die so far up in the mountains? Was he murdered? The many theories as to the cause of his death include battle, ritual sacrifice, bad weather, and starvation.

Both Austria and Italy claimed the Iceman. The dispute between the authorities of both countries over whose territory Ötzi had been discovered on continued until 1998. Then, after six years at the University of Innsbruck, the mummy was transferred to Italy. He now lies in a chamber at 21.2°F (-6°C) and 98 percent humidity in the South Tyrol Museum of Archaeology in Bolzano.

good-quality meat and wine were not available in the national capital, Vienna, which imports lamb from New Zealand. The farmer replied that Styrians did not export their lamb and wine. Selling his province's produce to his own country's capital was to him international trade!

Styrians who are not farmers are likely to be engaged in work related to one of the province's major industries: forestry, glass manufacturing, and the magnesite and iron and steel industries. Styria is the leading mining province in the nation, and its mining and steel industries have their scientific center in the Mining University in Leoben, north of Graz.

A hiker walks with a flock of sheep in Styria.

TYROLEANS

Around 728,500 Austrians live surrounded by majestic mountains in an area of nearly 5,000 square miles (12,950 sq km). This is Tyrol, the most visited region of Austria. Its capital, Innsbruck, is one of the country's most historic and renowned cities. The Austrian state of Tyrol is, curiously, divided into two parts which are separated by part of Salzburg.

Tourism is vitally important for the people of Tyrol, many of whom earn their living as hoteliers and mountain guides. The tourist industry has perhaps strengthened Tyrol's image as a land dominated by old farmhouses among Alpine peaks and forests.

The quaint village of Inneralpbach sits in the Alpbach Valley in Tyrol.

Tyroleans have retained a lot of their traditional ways, such as wearing their colorful folk clothing when performing folk dances. In a popular Tyrolean courtship dance, the man stamps his heels and slaps his knees as he circles his partner. Sometimes the male dancer may do somersaults and cartwheels and jump over the female dancer.

The village of Alpbach, about 37 miles (60 km) east of Innsbruck, sits on a plateau at an altitude of 3,281 feet (1,000 m). It has been called "Austria's most beautiful village" and "Europe's most beautiful flower village." Alpbach has a population of 2,300 people.

Famous for their traditions and nationalist fervor, Tyroleans are proud of their rich heritage as free and independent farmers who were never serfs to local nobility. Today, this history accounts for their strong sense of being Tyrolean as well as Austrian.

This identity is connected with the turbulent history of a province that has been fought over many times. The existence of silver mines plus the proximity of the Brenner Pass through the Alps to Italy made Tyrol a much disputed area. When Napoleon gave Tyrol to the king of Bavaria in the early nineteenth century, Tyroleans rose in revolt under the leadership of Andreas Hofer, who became an important folk hero.

CARINTHIANS

Situated in the Eastern Alps, Carinthia is the southernmost Austrian state and is noted for its mountains and lakes. Most Carinthians speak German. The minority language, Slovene, is spoken by the descendants of Slovenes who settled in the area centuries ago.

After World War I, when many Central and Eastern European boundaries shifted, and part of Hungary became Austria's and part of Tyrol became Italy's, Austria had to also give parts of Carinthia to Italy and to the then new nation of Yugoslavia. Today, many visitors to the Slovene capital of Ljubljana (LOO-blee-AH-nah) comment on the Austrian feel of that city.

Carinthia has a rich Celtic background. Europe's largest Celtic settlement, excavated at Magdalensberg, is an important archaeological site.

There are well over half a million Carinthians today, mostly farmers and mine workers. Cattle and sheep raising, corn, wheat, and fruit farming, and lignite, lead, and iron mining are major industries in Carinthia. There are plants manufacturing chemicals and textiles in both Klagenfurt, the capital of Carinthia, and Villach, an important industrial town and a major junction in the eastern Alps.

Kalgenfurt, the capital of Carinthia, is situated on the beautiful Alpine *Wörthersee* (Lake Wörth). *See* means "lake" in German.

Austria has produced many internationally known artists, musicians, scientists, great thinkers, entertainers, and other influential people. Just a few famous Austrians include:

Sigmund Freud

Wolfgang Amadeus Mozart

Sigmund Freud (1856–1939)—psychologist, "father of psychoanalysis," medical doctor, author

Franz Joseph Haydn (1732–1809)—musician, composer

Adolf Hitler (1889–1945)—born in Austria, German Nazi Party leader, chancellor, and dictator responsible for World War II and the Holocaust

Gustav Klimt (1862–1918)—Art Nouveau painter

Gregor Mendel (1822–1884)—monk, scientist known as the "father of modern genetics"

Wolfgang Amadeus Mozart (1756–1791)—child prodigy, considered one of the greatest composers of all time

Arnold Schwarzenegger (b. 1947)—bodybuilder, actor, former governor of California

Johann Strauss (1825–1899)—composer known as "The Waltz King"

Maria von Trapp (1905–1987)—singer, memoirist, the inspiration for The Sound of Music

Simon Wiesenthal (1908–2005)—Holocaust survivor, writer, Nazi hunter

PEOPLE OF VORARLBERG

Vorarlberg, the most westerly province, and the second smallest in the country, is bordered by the Arlberg Range in the east and opens into Switzerland and Germany in the west and north.

The German spoken in Vorarlberg sounds more like Swiss German than like the Austrian German heard in most parts of the country. That's not surprising; Zurich, the capital of Switzerland, is only an hour's drive away compared to a day's drive to Vienna. Both the Swiss and the people of Vorarlberg are descended from the ancient German Alemannic tribes that dominated central Europe in the third century BCE.

Vorarlberg has a population of 350,000 people, living mostly on the plains of the Rhine. The capital of this region is Bregenz. Vorarlberg is the most traditional province of Austria. The people are proud of the customs that are uniquely theirs, especially in the Bregenzerwald region, where people continue to live much as they did in the past. Another characteristic that unites the people in Vorarlberg is a love of nature that drives them to seek ways to live in harmony with the environment.

People stroll through a town square in Bregenz.

Young people relax in a park near City Hall in Vienna.

THE VIENNESE

Vienna is home to some 1,795,000 people. There are also significant Czech and Slovak communities and a large group of foreign workers, mostly from Slovenia.

The stereotype of the Viennese citizen is an elegant, sophisticated, artistic lover of classical music and cream pastries, who studies the newspaper for hours in a smart coffeehouse. As with so many aspects of Austrian culture, the explanation for this lies in history.

The Austrian Empire came to a sudden end after World War I, but imperial attitudes did not die as quickly. Vienna, the capital city of the former empire, had taken on a rich cosmopolitan character. It was the city most patronized by artists and intellectuals, and even its ordinary citizens had a sense of being the aristocrats of Austria.

The remnants of Austria's imperial past have lived on into the twenty-first century in the Viennese "attitude," which a farmer from Vorarlberg might dismiss as snobbery. But Viennese refer to *Landl* (LAHND-uhl), their name for Vorarlberg meaning "the little province," in a semi-affectionate way, for there is a big-city air in their perception of the agricultural province so far west.

The city's grand architecture is another manifestation of the people's attitude. The imperial Hofburg Palace, for example, occupies a large area in the old city and houses several museums.

The legacy of the past can also be seen in the Viennese telephone directory. One regularly comes across foreign-sounding names that are obviously not German. Viennese are proud of their rich cultural heritage. Most families in Vienna can claim a grandparent or great-grandparent of Czech or Hungarian descent.

The Hofburg Palace in Vienna

INTERNET LINKS

www.archaeologiemuseum.it/en
The South Tyrol Museum of Archaeology has a special section, in English, on Ötzi the Iceman.

www.austria.info/uk/service-facts/about-austria/famous-austrians
This site has a section on famous Austrians (mostly musicians).

www.austria.info/uk/service-facts/customs-and-expressions
This Austrian tourism site has some light-hearted articles on "Austrianness."

LIFESTYLE

A bench under a tree on Zwölferhorn Mountain provides a glorious view of Wolfgangsee, the lake far below.

7

MOST AUSTRIANS WOULD PROBABLY agree that they enjoy a high quality of life. In general, studies find that Austrians are more satisfied with their lives than are folks in most developed nations. Austrians seek to balance work and thrift with enjoyment of good food, wine, music, and conversation.

Hikers enjoy a mountain-climbing expedition.

In 2000, the World Health Organization (WHO) rated Austria's health care system as ninth best in the world. For comparison, France was rated number 1, the United States was rated number 37, and Myanmar came in last at number 190. All Austrians receive free publicly funded care, but they also have the option to purchase supplementary private health insurance.

Austrian men undergo compulsory military service lasting less than a year, with periods of retraining later. Nevertheless, Austrians do not see their army as an aggressive force. When communism in Europe collapsed in the 1990s, there were calls to disband the army altogether.

International political and social issues are common topics in two of the most popular locations for socializing in Austria: the coffeehouse and the wine tavern.

Austrian soldiers stand at attention in Vienna.

SOCIAL PARTNERSHIP

"Social partnership" is the term that describes the voluntary cooperation between employers and employees practiced in Austria. Trade union representatives meet behind closed doors with leaders of industry and commerce, and they thrash out matters of policy concerning changes in wages and prices. These meetings have no legal or constitutional basis, but compromises made at these meetings filter through to parliament and influence the decisions made there.

This social partnership reflects a new attitude toward economic and social life that emerged after World War II, and it is characteristic of the Austrian way of doing things. Issues that could lead to confrontation and bitterness are avoided, and compromise is seen as the best way of dealing with problems.

THE COFFEEHOUSE

The coffeehouse is not just a place for drinking coffee. Coffee drinking is a way of life for Austrians, whose love of coffee dates to the end of the

seventeenth century and the Turkish attack on Vienna. As the defeated Turks retreated in a hurry, they left behind hundreds of sacks filled with coffee beans. The Viennese initially had no idea what the brown beans were. It was an Austrian merchant who had traveled to Turkey who realized what could be done with them. He opened the first coffeehouse and experimented with the beans until he found a taste that the citizens could not resist.

The Viennese coffeehouse is a national institution. A typical cross-section of the capital's citizens will visit a coffeehouse during the course of the day. Office workers pop in for breakfast, students sit for hours with their textbooks, businesspeople talk shop, and shoppers stop by for a break.

Regular patrons will have their own table, such as newspaper addicts who systematically work their way through the racks of national and international publications provided for customers. Customers may order coffee once or several times, and the waiters keep serving fresh glasses of water unless another drink is ordered.

Outdoor diners enjoy coffee and pastries at Vienna's famous Café Mozart.

The *Schreiberhaus* (Schreiber House) in Vienna is a well-known heuriger tavern and restaurant.

THE HEURIGER

The *heuriger* (HI-ree-geh) is a unique kind of wine tavern commonly found in Vienna and eastern Austria. The word means "this year's," so strictly speaking, only new wines are served. This is indicated by a sprig of fir or pine or a wreath of holly placed over the door of the tavern.

Inside, Austrians sit around tables talking about both crucial and trivial matters with equal enthusiasm. There is usually both hot and cold food available buffet-style. In the larger heuriger, especially in the tourist areas, live music is played.

Visiting a heuriger is unlike visiting a wine bar in the United States. A visit to a heuriger is often a family occasion, when children and even pets are welcome. The wine may be served mixed with soda water; this is known as a *g'spritzter* (ges-SHPRIT-zer). With plenty of food available, it is not unusual for a group of friends to stay chatting and socializing all evening and night.

LIFE IN THE COUNTRYSIDE

Many rural families in Tyrol live in farmhouses that belonged to their ancestors. The farmhouse is typically made from stone and wood, with a bell tower to summon the men from the fields at lunchtime.

Roman Catholicism is more deeply ingrained in the countryside than in the cities. A crucifix on the farmhouse gable is common, or a painted inscription above the door, "We appreciate the good that Jesus Christ has done for us."

A typical farm occupies about 50 acres (20.24 ha) of woodland and pasture for half a dozen cows, several calves, a few pigs, and a dozen or more hens. The cows are taken into the Alps to graze in the summer and brought down again in late autumn.

In the past, rural Austrians spent harsh Alpine winters repairing tools, living on cheese and dried meat, and making handicrafts. The animals were kept indoors and fed hay.

Tourism now offers alternative employment during the winter months, especially in western Austria. Many farmers supplement their income with money spent by tourists. They convert the living room into a bedroom, and the kitchen takes over as the center of family life during the winter months. Then when the tourists leave, farming begins again—farming families loosen the soil and plant potatoes and corn.

Some families still make cheese, although it is probably the grandparents who possess the skill. Breadmaking is more common; a simple lunch can be made out of rye bread, or *roggenbrot* (ROGGEN-broht). After Mass every Sunday, the men may play a card game of *watten* (VAH-tehn), over a jug of beer at the local beer hall.

A mother and son harvest potatoes.

EDUCATION

School is compulsory in Austria, and all schools are coeducational. Every child between six and ten years of age attends a *volksschule* (folks-SHOO-leh), or elementary school. After that, some 80 percent of elementary school students are directed into *hauptschulen* (howpt-SHOO-len), or general secondary schools. The remaining minority enroll in the more prestigious gymnasium, or *allgemeinbildende höhere schulen* (AHL-geh-mine-BIL-dent-deh HOE-heh-reh SHOO-len), or AHS, an upper-level secondary school that focuses on academics.

All students must take another language, usually English, French, Spanish, or Italian. After elementary education it is also possible to pursue vocational training by attending the medium-level or higher-level technical schools. Students attend these schools for careers in fields such as industry, agriculture, forestry, nursing, tourism, and social work.

From either an upper-level technical school or AHS, students can enter one of the country's twenty-three public or thirteen private universities, including six art colleges. Many of Austria's universities have a long history. The University of Vienna, for example, was founded in 1365, and is the oldest university in German-speaking Europe. Universities in Graz and Innsbruck were founded in the sixteenth and seventeenth centuries respectively. Graz and Vienna boast prestigious technical universities.

The Vienna University of Economic and Business Library and Learning Center has bold architectural lines.

There are equal opportunities for all Austrians to receive an education. Children of foreign workers have the same right to free education as Austria-born children. Every student has access to free textbooks and free transportation to and from school.

SOCIAL SECURITY

Austria has one of the best social welfare systems in the world. Compulsory national health insurance covers the medical expenses of visits to the doctor or stays in a hospital. Similarly, workers are protected against financial loss in the event of sickness or an accident.

Social insurance also covers the self-employed, including farmers. Street entertainers can also be considered self-employed, although some sociologists call what they do "disguised begging."

Unemployment benefits average nearly half the previous normal earnings, although such benefits are not paid out indefinitely. Even in the case of death, benefits include a contribution to funeral expenses.

There are thirteen legal holidays in the Austrian calendar, and workers receive five weeks of paid vacation each year. The elderly are very well taken care of. Retired Austrians are entitled to old-age pensions. Men retire at age sixty-five; women at age sixty. (Women's retirement age is set to increase to age sixty-five between 2024 and 2033.) The disabled also receive pensions, regardless of age.

All these benefits are financed by a combination of employers' and employees' contributions plus government funds. With more than a quarter of the proceeds of its economic growth paying for social security, Austria can justly claim to be one of the most advanced of welfare states.

THE AUSTRIAN LIFE CYCLE

In a country where 63.4 percent of the population are Roman Catholics, baptism is one of the earliest rites of passage for the individual. Parents bring their babies to the church where the priest performs a simple ceremony to initiate the baby into the Roman Catholic faith. Relatives and friends attend the ceremony to witness the event.

Marriage for practicing Catholics is a church affair. After the wedding ceremony, the couple leaves on their honeymoon, which often means a visit to another European country, if the couple can afford it.

Funerals are church affairs as well. Before the day of the funeral, the body is laid out for family and friends to pay their last respects. On the day of the funeral, a ceremony is held in the church, followed by a ceremony at the graveyard as the coffin is lowered into the ground.

In the countryside, where old traditions and customs have survived relatively intact, there are rites originating in the passing of the seasons: the end of winter and the advent of spring is marked by carnivals and processions, and during the fall, there are thanksgiving ceremonies and country fairs.

Some parades still observed today have their origins in pre-Christian times. For example, during the "ghosts' parade," men dressed in costumes and large wooden masks glide through the streets in an eerie procession—a throwback to the days of pagan spirit worship.

TRADITIONAL DRESS

The most characteristic Austrian traditional dress for women is the dirndl, consisting of an embroidered blouse with a lace bodice worn over a full skirt and an apron. Men wear *lederhosen* ("LAY-der-HOH-sen"), or leather shorts, with ornamental suspenders and belts. They also wear distinctive hats and short jackets without lapels.

Austrians now generally wear their traditional clothes only for festive and tourist occasions. They maintain the authentic uniqueness of their traditional dress by observing the strict regional differences in individual items. The style of the hats, for example, varies not just from one region to another but even from one valley to another. Headgear for women is sometimes very distinctively braided with gold. A woman's hat from Vorarlberg, instead of resting on the head, rises from it and looks as if it is being worn upside down.

Traditional clothes in the Salzkammergut region in central Austria resemble those of eighteenth-century European ladies and gentlemen, with the men donning long jackets and white socks pulled up to the knee and tied with a colored ribbon.

A couple in traditional garb stand in an Alpine meadow.

INTERNET LINKS

www.aboutaustria.org
This travel site has sections on Austrian etiquette, quality of life, and other lifestyle topics.

www.kwintessential.co.uk/resources/global-etiquette/austria-country-profile.html
Although this site is geared toward business travelers, it gives a quick overview of the Austrian lifestyle.

www.thelovelyplanet.net/traditional-dress-of-austria-dirndl-lederhosen-and-tracht
See lots of photos of Austrian traditional dress on this site.

RELIGION

The picturesque old town in Salzburg is a World Heritage site.

THE BEAUTIFUL CATHEDRALS, churches, and monasteries of Austria proclaim the country's rich Roman Catholic background. There was a time, back in the 1950s, when the country regained independence, when 90 percent of the population were baptized Catholics. Since then the nation's religious profile has shifted, reflecting the changing times. Austria is still a predominantly Roman Catholic country, but only 63.4 percent of the population profess that faith, according to the 2012 census. A mere 3.8 percent are Protestants.

Church and State were one until the fall of the Hapsburg Empire, but they are now separate. Austria's constitutional foundations guarantee freedom of religion, as well as the freedom to have no religion. Austria's government and legal system are religiously neutral. For example, divorce and abortion are legally possible even though the Catholic Church does not agree with it. Nevertheless, the state allows recognized churches and religious groups to collect a "church tax" of 1.1 percent of a person's income. Only the Catholic Church takes advantage of that proviso, and the church tax is compulsory for all Catholics in Austria.

8

The oldest monastery in Austria is St. Peter's Abbey in Salzburg. The Benedictine monastery was founded in 696 CE and has been in continuous operation since then.

MONASTERIES

The Cistercians are an order of monks renowned for their strict austerity. During the great spread of monastic houses in the eleventh and twelfth centuries, the Cistercians moved into Austria. They settled on formerly unproductive land and worked very hard as agriculturalists. In time, they grew wealthy and split into two branches. One branch retained the original strict rules, while the other had fewer restrictions.

The Stams Cisterian Abbey in Tyrol was built in 1273.

As Austria remained Roman Catholic, the Cistercians did not suffer as badly during the Protestant Reformation as did their counterparts in other countries in Europe, when Roman Catholic churches and monasteries came under attack. When the Protestant Reformation penetrated Austria in the sixteenth century, the monarchy and the majority of the population kept their faith.

Cistercian monasteries in Austria that were founded in the twelfth century still function today, and the monks still wear the same white dark-collared cassock and black scapula. Many of the abbeys have survived by converting part of the building into a private school or by leasing out the surrounding farmland.

CHOICE OF RELIGION

Austrian law on the people's choice of religious education for children is very liberal. Every young person age fourteen and older can freely choose his or her religion. The state pays for religious education for every child, regardless of faith.

If the child is ten years old or younger, the parents have the right to choose the child's religion. For children between ages ten and twelve, the parents still have the final say, although the child has to be consulted. Between ages twelve and fourteen, a child's religion cannot be changed against his or her will. Once a child reaches age fourteen, he or she is deemed to be "of full legal age" where religious matters are concerned and can choose his or her religion freely and independently.

ROMAN CATHOLICISM

Christianity came to Austria during the time of the Roman Empire. By the third century CE, it had spread widely. Austria's Roman Catholic roots can be traced back to missionaries who founded monasteries in the fifth and sixth centuries. In the seventh century, a diocese founded at Salzburg and another at Passau became centers for the Christianization of southern and eastern Austria. Between the tenth and thirteenth centuries, many monasteries were founded with the encouragement of Austria's rulers. The major monastic orders were the Augustinians, Benedictines, Premonstratensians, and Cistercians. Much later, in the sixteenth century, other religious orders included the Jesuits, Capuchins, Barnabites, and Servites.

During World War II, the Catholic Church played an officially neutral role. Nevertheless, the Church's record during that time is spotty, with evidence of

Stephansdom, or St. Stephen's Cathedral, is the most important religious building in Vienna.

Dissatisfaction with the Roman Catholic Church has not only been felt by Austrian parishioners but by some of the clergy as well. In 2006, the Austrian priest Father Helmut

Schüller founded a group of dissident Catholic priests with his "Call to Disobedience." The organization favors radical reforms to church structure and principles, including opening up the priesthood to women and married men, and doing away with the clergy's celibacy requirement. The group also supports gay marriage, and allowing lay people to conduct communion services without a priest. All of these positions are currently forbidden by the Catholic Church. Schüller says he believes these reforms would restore vitality to the Catholic Church.

The Call to Disobedience movement, sometimes called the Austrian Priests' Initiative, has caused a great schism in the Austrian Church. In 2011, Pope Benedict responded to Schüller by removing his title of Monsignor, an honorific granted by the Catholic Church, but did not revoke his standing as a priest. Pope Francis, Benedict's successor, while not endorsing the group's positions, has been more open to dialogue about change.

both support for and resistance against the Nazis. In Austria, as elsewhere, Catholics were subjected to oppression and persecution by the regime.

Today, even though active participation in the Church has been in decline for several decades, most Austrians have a Catholic background and their lives reflect Catholic traditions and culture.

Roman Catholicism is traditionally practiced in the countryside more than in the cities, where people who profess to be Roman Catholic might not necessarily observe the religion strictly in their daily lives.

OTHER RELIGIONS

Today, the Austrian government legally recognizes thirteen churches and religious communities. Buddhism, for example, was recognized in 1983 and today has about ten thousand followers, mostly in Vienna. Indeed, Vienna is more diverse in matters of religion than is any other part of Austria. Other faiths are more evident in the capital city than elsewhere in the country.

The Evangelical Church of Villach on a sunny winter morning.

PROTESTANTISM   Protestants in Austria belong mainly to the Lutheran and Reformed churches. Most live in Burgenland. In 1781, Emperor Joseph II signed the Deed of Tolerance, allowing Protestants to build chapels and appoint pastors. In 1861 Emperor Franz Joseph I signed the Deed of Protestants, giving Protestants the freedom to practice their faith in public. Protestants were finally entitled to equal civic rights in such areas as education and social welfare.

JUDAISM   The Jews in Vienna can trace their history in Austria to the tenth century. The Jews played a vital role in the cultural life of the capital, especially at the turn of the twentieth century. After World War II, only a few hundred of the original 180,000 Jews remained in Vienna as a result of the Nazis' "Final Solution"—Hitler's policy of systematically exterminating the Jewish population. Today there are about seven thousand Jews in Vienna.

The Islamic
Center of Vienna
in Bruckhaufen,
Vienna, was built in
1979 by King Faisal
of Saudi Arabia.

ISLAM Muslims are the fastest-growing religious group, mainly due to the influx of Muslims from Turkey, the Balkans, and the Middle East. In 2014, statistics showed that Muslim students outnumbered Roman Catholic students at middle and secondary schools in Vienna. Austria was the first European country to officially recognize Islam, which it did in 1912 following the 1908 Austria-Hungary annexation of Bosnia-Herzegovina. (Of course, the breakup of the Austria Hungry Empire nullified that recognition, but Islam remained an established religion in Austria throughout its various incarnations throughout the twentieth century.)

The vast majority of Muslims in Austria today are Sunnis. Most came to the country in the 1960s as migrant workers from Turkey and Bosnia. Austria has the highest percentage of Muslim population of all the European countries. The new wave of mostly Muslim migrants and asylum seekers in 2015 that swept through Europe will likely affect that population.

In 2015, the Austrian parliament passed an *Islamgesetz* (Islam Law) banning the foreign funding of mosques and imam salaries. It also regulates which version of the Qur'an may be used in Austria. These restrictions are designed to combat the spread of radical Islam. However, the law also gives Muslims additional rights, such as the rights to halal (religiously approved) food and pastoral care in the military.

NONE OR OTHER   The second-largest category, 22 percent, of religious choice marked by Austrians in the 2012 census was "None or Other." This follows a general trend across Europe to secularism, as well as dissatisfaction with the policies of the Catholic Church. However, this selection is also thought to reflect a desire among some Austrians to avoid the church tax.

Karlskirche (St. Charles's Church), a magnificent baroque church in Vienna, is illuminated at night.

INTERNET LINKS

www.austria.org/religion
The site of the Austrian Embassy in Washington, DC, explains Austria's religious landscape.

www.tourmycountry.com/austria/monasteries.htm
This is an overview of the abbeys, convents, and monasteries of Austria.

www.virtualvienna.net/living-in-vienna/religion
This site offers a brief overview of the main religions in Austria, with the focus on Vienna.

LANGUAGE

A billboard in Graz, the capital of Styria, shows native Arnold Schwarzenegger when he was elected governor of California. It reads "Real. Strong. Styrian!"

9

WHEN IT COMES TO LANGUAGE, there is no such thing as Austrian. Given Austria's long, shared cultural and political history with Germany, it's not surprising that its people speak German. In fact, Austria is the only country—apart from Germany, of course—where German is the national language. Yet German is one of the main languages of the Western world. It is spoken by more than a hundred million people. There are German-speaking communities across the globe, from Russia to Latin America.

Austrian German does not sound the same as the German spoken in Germany. It's possible to distinguish Austrians from Germans by the way they pronounce the words. (The situation is analogous to the difference between British English and American English. People in the United States do not speak "American"; rather, because of their history, they speak English. However, there are significant differences, in both words and pronunciation, between English English and American English. The same is true of the English spoken in England, Scotland, and Ireland.)

Two general divisions of the German language are High German and Low German, having their origins in the southern highlands and northern lowlands of Germany respectively. While High German is the standard

The differences between German and Austrian speech differ slightly but recognizably. There is an often-heard saying that goes something like this: "In Berlin they will tell you that the situation is serious but not desperate; in Vienna they will tell you that it is desperate but not serious."

written form and the medium for official communication in Germany, Austria's equivalent is High Austrian German, which is the "official" form of German used in the country.

While 98 percent of the Austrian population speak German, the minority groups have their own languages as well. Slovenian is spoken in southern Carinthia, and Croatian and Hungarian are used in Burgenland.

AUSTRIAN GERMAN

Not only is the German spoken in Austria different from the language of Germany, but the German spoken in one part of Austria is different from that spoken in another part. The dialects in Austria are more distinct than those in Germany. A dialect speaker from Vorarlberg, for instance, could have some difficulty conversing with a local speaker from eastern Austria. In the mountainous areas of western Austria, it is often the

Daily newspapers on a stand in Vienna are in several languages.

case that the inhabitants of one valley have a separate dialect from those living in another valley only a few miles away.

The German spoken in Vorarlberg is very similar to the German used in neighboring Switzerland. This is because the people in this region have common roots in the Alemannic tribes that occupied this part of central Europe in the seventh century.

On the other hand, Vienna's dialect, Wienerisch (VEE-ner-ish), has developed its own unique identity. A Tyrolean will recognize Wienerisch as quickly as a Californian will detect Bostonian speech. One feature of Wienerisch is the affix *erl*, which changes nouns into diminutives. For example, the word for "kiss" in High German is *kuss* (koos), but in Wienerisch it becomes *busserl* (BOOS-serl).

Generally, Austrian German is softer than that of Germany. While Germans say "KAH-fay" for coffee, Austrians say "kah-FAY." While Germans say *guten morgen* (meaning "good morning") with a pronounced stress on certain syllables (GOO-ten MOR-gen), Austrians allow the sounds to flow more easily into one another and the sharpness is softened (goo-ten MOR-gen).

For a long time German was written in a Gothic style known as Fraktur (FRAHK-toor), which originated in the fourteenth century. Fraktur has been replaced by standardized Roman characters that make reading and speaking German a lot easier.

However, Roman characters are not pronounced the same way in German as they are in English. There are some rules of pronunciation that a person learning German for the first time needs to get acquainted with in order to read the letters and letter combinations correctly.

LETTER(S)	SOUND	EXAMPLE
j	"y"	ja, *which means yes, is pronounced* "ya."
sch	"sh"	Schnee, *which means snow, is pronounced* "shnee."
sp	"shp"	sprechen, *which means speak, is pronounced* "shprek-ken."
st	"sht"	Strasse, *which means street, is pronounced* "shtrah-seh."
w	"v"	Raymond Weil *is pronounced Raymond* "Veil."
v	"f"	vier, *which means four, is pronounced* "fier."

GERMAN COMPOUNDS

"An average sentence, in a German newspaper, is a sublime and impressive curiosity; it occupies a quarter of a column ... it is built mainly of compound words constructed by the writer on the spot, and not to be found in any dictionary—six or seven words compacted into one, without joint or seam ... German books are easy enough to read when you hold them before the looking-glass or stand on your head—so as to reverse the construction—but I think that to learn to read and understand a German newspaper is a thing which must always remain an impossibility to a foreigner."

—Mark Twain
"The Awful German Language" (1880)

The American writer Mark Twain often poked fun at the German language. In the excerpt above, he comments on the ability of Germans to join words

Early in the Christian era, many Germanic tribes mass-migrated, with some ending up in Britain, where they had a decisive influence on the English language. In fact, English is a Germanic language and there are many similarities between the two vocabularies. These German words are spelled the same and mean the same in English:

blind   finger   ring   butter   hand   warm

Some of the words above begin with a capital letter in German. One unusual characteristic about written German is that all nouns begin with a capital letter.

Other words are so similar, although spelled and pronounced a little differently, that the link between the two languages is clear:

GERMAN	ENGLISH
Vater (FAH-ter)	father
Mütter (MOO-ter)	mother
Fisch (fish)	fish
gut (goot)	good
Buch (book)	book
Gott (got)	God
Freund (FRAH-eend)	friend

The following German words have entered the English language:

kindergarten (KEEN-DAR-gar-TEN)	kindergarten
lager (LA-GER)	light beer
poodle (POOD-el)	a small furry dog
hinterland (HEEN-ter-LAAND)	backcountry, wilderness
blitzkrieg (blitz-KREEG)	a sudden heavy attack, shortened to blitz

to form new words. This can sometimes produce extremely long words or compounds. For example, the compound word *Volksschullehrerseminar* (FOLKS-SHOOL-lay-rer-SEMINAR) is made up of these words: *volks* ("people or public"), *schul* ("school"), *lehrer* ("teacher"), and *seminar* ("seminary").

Put them together and you get a "public school teachers' seminary," or in everyday English, a "training college for public school teachers."

Sometimes the compounding can stretch anyone's linguistic ability. Try reading aloud one of the longest German words, the title for the captain of a steamboat on the Danube River: *Donaudampfschiffahrtsgesellschaftskapitän* (DON-au-DAMPF-SHEEF-arts-GASAL-shaft-KAPITAN). The words making up this compound word are: *Donau* (the Danube), *dampf* (steam), *schiff* (ship), *fahrt* (trip or journey), *gesellschaft* (company), and *kapitän* (captain).

MINORITY LANGUAGES

In Burgenland, the Croatian minority is trying to preserve their language and culture. One area of dispute has been the provision of bilingual place names. According to the Austrian constitution, the rights of the Slovene and Croatian minorities are guaranteed. The 1976 Ethnic Groups Act provides for the rights of Croats, Hungarians, Slovenes, Romanies, Czechs, and Slovaks. However, provisions for bilingual place names still depend on whether the minority group makes up at least one-quarter of the population in the area. This condition makes it difficult for minorities to preserve their culture and language, and the issue remains unresolved. For example, in Carinthia, where Slovenes make up only 4 percent of the province's population, the Slovene people are fighting to keep the non-German names of their villages.

INTERNET LINKS

www.omniglot.com/writing/german.htm
Omniglot offers a good basic introduction to German.

www.youtube.com/watch?v=m6uwN-rxEgc
www.youtube.com/watch?v=SkuAd97WUSw
"Austrian German vs German German," Parts I and II, are cute, short videos highlighting the difference between the two kinds of German.

ARTS

Musicians play at the Villacher *Kirchtag*, the largest traditional folk festival in Austria.

10

FROM CLASSICAL MUSIC TO yodeling, music runs in the blood of many Austrians. The eighteenth and nineteen centuries were a golden age for Austrian music, and Vienna was the classical music center of Europe. It would have been rare during that time to find a middle-class Viennese family that could not put together its own string quartet.

Folk musicians wear traditional costumes at the annual Villacher festival.

"If it is true that I have talent, I owe it, above everything else, to my beloved city of Vienna ... in whose soul is rooted my whole strength, in whose air float the melodies which my ear has caught, my heart has drunk in, and my hand has written down."
—Johann Strauss, writing about his waltz music

Today, Austrians are just as likely to be into jazz, electronica, pop, rock, or hip hop, but they nevertheless revere their country's extraordinary musical legacy. Some of the greatest composers of all time—Haydn, the Johann Strausses, Mozart, Schubert, Schönberg, and Bruckner—were all Austrians.

VIENNA'S MUSICAL HERITAGE

Any roll call of the world's greatest classical composers will include more musicians from Vienna than from any other city. The music of Vienna had a decisive effect on the form of the symphony and the string quartet, and the city became the center for new symphonic writing. Beethoven settled in Vienna to work as a composer, as did Brahms. Gustav Mahler and Richard Strauss, though not Austrian by birth, are also considered a major part of the country's musical heritage.

Music continues to play an important role in the lives of Austrians—from music for the folk dances of Tyrol to the studied elegance of performances by the Vienna Philharmonic Orchestra and the Vienna State Opera.

The Vienna Boys' Choir performs the "Christmas in Vienna" concert in 2014.

FRANZ JOSEPH HAYDN (1732-1809)

Haydn lived in Burgenland in relative comfort and ease under the patronage of two wealthy Hungarian princes. Haydn was in his time the music idol of the European intelligentsia. He made two famous trips to London and Ireland, winning great acclaim.

Haydn was interested in the structure of music and is credited with shaping the symphony into its present form. He is often called the "father of the symphony" and the "father of the string quartet."

Haydn used folk dance music in his compositions. His Emperor Quartet *(1797), composed for the Austrian national anthem during the monarchy, has its musical origins in a foot-stomping dance for farmers. The dance rhythms are recognizable at the beginning and end of the piece. He also used the rustic country waltz, the* landler *(LAHND-leh), in his symphonies and in his oratorio,* The Creation *(1798), which is considered his masterpiece.*

Franz Joseph Haydn conducts a string quartet.

Two of Austria's most important musical institutions are the Vienna Philharmonic Orchestra and the Vienna Boys' Choir. The orchestra was founded in 1842 and plays music from the classical and Romantic periods. It is the world's last major orchestra to admit women; one harpist is its only female member. The choir consists of boys between the ages of eight and thirteen and has been singing for the morning Mass in the Hofburg Chapel for five hundred years. The choir often does international performances as well.

THE WALTZ

The waltz, initially known as the landler, has its origin in Austria as a traditional dance in which partners come together in each other's arms, then turn with a hop and a step.

Dancers waltz in this ink drawing from nineteenth-century Austria.

Schubert was born in Vienna and never left the city except for brief excursions in the countryside. As a member of the choir of the Imperial Court Chapel, he received the

best education available in Vienna. He was dismissed from the choir in 1813 when his voice changed. As he was too short for military service, he became a schoolteacher like his father.

Schubert composed songs, operettas, and choral pieces. He also wrote symphonies, piano sonatas, chamber music, and dance pieces for the piano. Some of his best-known music includes The Erlking—*the tragic ride of a father trying to outdistance Death—and* The Trout.

Schubert was a great admirer of Beethoven. When Schubert died in November 1828, he was buried close to Beethoven. The remains of the two composers were reburied side by side in 1863. The newspapers in Vienna ignored Schubert while he was alive but printed memorial poems about him when he died. Often dismissed as only a songwriter, Schubert showed his versatility in his symphonies, sonatas, and quartets.

The waltz gained the interest of the upper classes, but because they were always dressed fashionably for court appearances, the waltz was gradually modified to fit their dress, which was restrictive and prevented them from moving quickly enough when they danced. Also, the ballroom floors were smooth, unlike the stone floors on which the dance was born. This too encouraged a slower waltz.

But an important element of the dance remained—close physical contact in three-four time. As the waltz became fashionable across Europe, it

Mozart was born in Salzburg. His parents, Leopold and Anna Maria, had six other children, five of whom died in infancy. Only Mozart and his sister Maria Anna survived, both musically gifted.

Mozart excelled in every musical medium of his time and is recognized as Europe's most universal composer. At age three, he played the harpsichord and took to the violin without any formal training. He composed his first symphony at age eight and gained fame as a child prodigy while touring Europe.

Despite an auspicious childhood and obvious talent, Mozart was not appreciated by the Archbishop of Salzburg, for whom he worked. He angered the archbishop when he declared that he, the musician, "probably had more nobility than a count." Constant quarrels eventually led to his dismissal.

Mozart traveled across Europe to find work. He was once appointed the Imperial and Royal Chamber Composer for the Hapsburg emperor Joseph II. But the grand title meant little, as Mozart was underpaid and soon fell into debt.

Constant travel took a toll on Mozart's health. He died at age thirty-five in Salzburg, singing strains from his last work, Requiem. *In his short life, Mozart had composed fifty symphonies, twenty-two operas, and innumerable other works. His music is best known for its gaiety, though it has a melancholic strain and reflects the spirit of the Enlightenment. His opera* The Marriage of Figaro *tells the tale of the struggle between a master and a servant and celebrates the dignity of the common man.*

Mozart's genius was not fully appreciated in his lifetime. Legend says that he died in poverty and his wife had no money to pay for his funeral. Mozart was buried in a pauper's grave, the exact location of which remains unknown. But his music has since won acclaim all over the world.

provoked critics. In 1818 the *Times* newspaper of London labeled the waltz "that indecent foreign dance" and called on parents to be wary of the moral danger of "so fatal a contagion," even though partners in a waltz then did not dance as close to each other as people do in a waltz today. It was not until the end of the nineteenth century that people began to dance in the close embrace that now characterizes the waltz.

The most enduring and most famous pieces of waltz music were composed by Johann Strauss and his son Johann Strauss Jr. in the nineteenth century. Johann Sr. composed more than 150 waltzes, as well as music for other dance forms during his time. Johann Jr. immortalized Vienna with his famous waltz, *The Blue Danube*. When his father died, he took over the orchestra and gained even greater fame than Johann Sr. had. The younger Strauss toured as far as the United States and Russia. He also wrote operettas and other dance music. When he died, the entire "dancing Vienna" era also came to an end. A golden statue of Johann Jr. stands in Stadtpark in Vienna.

A golden statue of Johann Strauss in Vienna's Stadtpark expresses Austrians' great esteem for the composer.

The Vienna State Opera, regarded by most Austrians as the country's cultural showcase, is a state-run institution that receives substantial subsidies every year.

In addition to the annual Opera Ball, the opera house stages about three hundred performances in one season. The Vienna Philharmonic Orchestra plays in the pit of the opera house, and the performances are possibly of the highest standard in the world.

The opera house was almost completely destroyed in World War II. It was rebuilt soon after and reopened in 1955. Today it is one of the most resplendent opera houses in the world. Yet despite its grandeur, the Vienna State Opera provides for shoestring-budget opera fans as well. Visitors can buy inexpensive standing-room tickets and stand on a graded floor with railings to lean on.

Perhaps the Vienna State Opera's greatest artistic director was Salzburg-born Herbert von Karajan (1908–1989), one of the world's foremost operatic conductors. A child prodigy at the piano, Karajan studied music at the Mozarteum University in Salzburg. He turned his attention to conducting when he was eighteen years old. After graduating from the Vienna Music Academy, Karajan made his conducting debut at the Vienna State Opera in 1937 and later became its artistic director.

TWENTIETH-CENTURY MUSIC

Austria's most revolutionary composer in the twentieth century was Arnold Schönberg (1874—1951). Starting out as a self-taught composer, he went on to produce the single most important innovation in post-classical music. With his *Three Piano Pieces* op. 11 of 1909, Schönberg created a new dimension of tonality, a method of composing that used twelve interrelated notes. In the twelve-tone system, the composer uses any twelve consecutive tones or notes in any order before repeating any one tone or note. Schönberg's works demonstrate an understanding of classical notions of form and technique but abandon conventional harmony.

Arnold Schoenberg in 1922.

EDUCATING NEW MUSICIANS

Austria's rich musical heritage continues to flourish. Music is a compulsory subject in elementary and secondary schools. Fifteen- to eighteen-year-olds in school have two hours of music instruction each week that can only be replaced in their last two years by art studies.

A large proportion of children are enrolled in private music schools to learn an instrument, and there are advanced classes at the various private conservatories in the provincial capitals. The most advanced training is available at the three music academies in Vienna, Salzburg, and Graz. These are public institutions organized like universities but quite independent of them. At the academies in Vienna and Salzburg, up to 50 percent of the students may be foreigners, especially Americans.

ART AND ARCHITECTURE

The development of architecture in Austria owes a lot to the monks who founded monasteries and abbeys in the country and who were wealthy enough to commission large-scale projects. Early architecture in Austria exhibited the Romanesque style, following Roman models of building with massive walls to carry the weight of rounded arches and vaults.

With the rise of the Gothic style in Europe, architects began designing taller buildings, using pointed arches and stone ribs to form the vaults. Outer walls helped take the downward thrust of these high arches. Projecting from the outer walls were curved bridges connected to the arches. The bridges extended, or "flew," to the ground to take the lateral thrust of the arches, thus they were called "flying" buttresses.

This design resulted in more spacious interiors and larger windows, which in turn encouraged the use of stained glass. Gothic-style churches, with their high pointed arches that rose toward the heavens, were the product of a combination of spiritual devotion and artistic skill.

Over the centuries, as vaults grew higher, the artwork became more elaborate. Doorways were carved and sculptures added, first in wood and later in stone. St. Stephen's Cathedral in Vienna, for example, which had its own workshop for sculptors, started out as a Romanesque building and was later restyled Gothic. The original building had thirty thousand wooden beams supporting the roof, but in 1945, after World War II, it had to be rebuilt due to the damage it sustained from bombing.

Architects and sculptors were kept busy by the Catholic Church. At a time when religion dominated so many forms of artistic expression, painters were also commissioned to add color to elaborately-carved altars.

In the seventeenth century, the Gothic style of architecture gave birth to the Italian-influenced baroque. The best of many examples in Austria of this opulent style is the abbey at Melk, originally a Benedictine abbey but rebuilt in the eighteenth century in the baroque style.

The center of Vienna is an architectural treat all by itself. The ring road around the city center is the site of several important buildings, each built in a different style toward the end of the nineteenth century. The parliament building resembles a Greek temple, while the university has the style of an Italian Renaissance palace. The city hall is more Gothic and Flemish in character. The most impressive of all is the Vienna State Opera, though legend has it that the building was so severely criticized when it was built that one of its architects committed suicide while the other died of a heart attack.

Vienna was also home to a thriving community of visual artists. One of the most well-known was Gustav Klimt (1862—1918). A prominent member

The Melk Abbey, a baroque-style Benedictine monastery built between 1702 and 1736, overlooks the Danube River in the Wachau Valley.

Special architectural wonders include the castles and homes of the aristocrats of the Hapsburg era. A schloss (shloss) is a castle or noble's residence; a lustschloss (LOOST-shloss) is an aristocrat's summer or winter holiday home; and a jagdschloss (YAHG-shloss) is a medieval-looking hunting lodge, with wooden beams, four-poster beds, suits of armor standing in the corners, and antlers hanging on the walls.

Many of these residences and lodges have been converted into hotels. A few, such as the Hapsburg hunting lodge at Mayerling, are now chapels. The palaces in Vienna have become famous museums, preserving within their gilded and ornate rococo walls the splendor and richness of Austria's imperial past.

Karmel-Mayerling, once an imperial hunting lodge, is now a Carmelite convent.

of the Vienna Succession movement, his paintings were unconventional, decorative, allegorical, and sometimes erotic. His "Golden Phase" produced some of his most popular work. In these paintings, Klimt applied gold leaf to the canvas to produce a shimmering effect. In 2006, his painting *Adele Bloch-Bauer I* (1907) sold for a record $135 million in New York City.

In 1897, a group of architects, painters, and designers formed the *Wiener Werkstätte* (Vienna Workshops) to produce arts and crafts. The idea was to apply a modernist art aesthetic to everyday objects. The artisans included metalworkers, leatherworkers, bookbinders, and woodworkers. The range of product lines included furniture, textiles, leather goods, enamel, jewelry, postcards, and ceramics.

INTERNET LINKS

www.austria.info/us/activities/culture-traditions/music-in-austria
This travel site covers a broad range of music in Austria, past and present.

www.iklimt.com
This site has an excellent interactive presentation about Gustav Klimt, his life and work.

www.leopoldmuseum.org/en
The Leopold Museum in Vienna focuses on Austrian artists, and its site has presentations on Klimt, Wiener Werkstätte, Vienna 1900 & Art Nouveau, and more.

artsbeat.blogs.nytimes.com/2011/01/10/top-10-composers-the-vienna-four/?_r=0
This *New York Times* blog presents an excellent series called "Top 10 Composers: The Vienna Four" (Mozart, Haydn, Beethoven, and Schubert) with video.

LEISURE

Gold medalist Michaela Dorfmeister of Austria celebrates her triumph in the Alpine skiing ladies downhill event in 2006 Winter Olympics in Italy.

11

PERHAPS NOT EVERY AUSTRIAN IS a skier, but it can seem that way. Like many residents of mountainous countries, Austrians love the outdoors and take sports seriously. Skiing, the national sport, is so popular that a public opinion poll once suggested that a majority of Austrians ranked the current champion skier as more of a national hero than Wolfgang Amadeus Mozart. When not skiing themselves, Austrians are avid spectators of the sport, with ski races held regularly on the glaciers of the Grossglockner and the slopes around Innsbruck.

Apart from skiing, playing and watching soccer are also very popular pastimes, and the Austrian national team is usually an able contender for the World Cup. In the summer, hiking is popular. With 35,000 miles (56,327 km) of mountain paths, there is room for everyone. Austria has one of the largest unspoiled landscapes in Western Europe, and this has a lot to do with the people's interest in walking. There are many routes traversing valleys, hills, and snow-clad mountains. Waterskiing and sailing on Austria's many lakes are other popular sports.

"It would be arrogant to say I knew I was going to win. But if I was full of doubts before, today I had no doubts. I had the voices of a thousand little gnomes in my head telling me this would be my day."
—Michaela Dorfmeister, Austrian ski champion, on winning the Olympic gold in February 2006

SKIING

Austrians are introduced to skiing as early as age three, so it is not surprising that it is their favorite sport. School trips will almost certainly include a skiing holiday at some point, either during the main season between November and April or in the off-season, at one of the year-round resorts above 11,000 feet (3,350 m). All the centers have professional instructors for all levels, from beginners to experts.

For a long time downhill skiing had been the most popular form, but now cross-country skiing, called *langlauf* (LAHNG-lauf), is gaining appeal. Many of the downhill slopes are getting crowded, and cross-country skiing takes one away from the crowds. It is also safer and less expensive. There are no great technical hurdles to overcome, and the beginner is spared the discouraging embarrassment of frequently falling over in the snow. The valley resorts have cross-country trails with loops and direct routes from one point to another.

A mother teaches her toddler son to ski.

Austria is one of the leading skiing nations in the world. Of all the Olympic gold medals Austria has won, perhaps more than half are for skiing, and the champions who win these titles become household names. But skiing is more than just a sport in Austria; it is also an industry. Austria's ski manufacturing industry is the largest in the world, with exports accounting for the bulk of sales.

Ski tourists are attracted to Austria's ski resorts, many of which are internationally famous. Visitors find Austria's ski resorts less impersonal than many of the resorts in Switzerland and Germany and appreciate the Austrian art of *gemütlichkeit* (geh-MOOT-likh-keit), an attitude that creates a leisurely, warm, and friendly atmosphere. Austrians and tourists are also drawn to the variety of activities offered in the bigger ski resorts, such as sleigh rides, tobogganing, and even yodeling.

THE HERMINATOR

One of the most famous Austrian skiers of recent times is Hermann Maier (b. 1972). He ranks among the finest Alpine ski racers in history, with four overall World Cup titles, two Olympic medals (both in 1998), and three World Championship titles.

He earned his nickname, "the Herminator," thanks to his seeming indestructibility. (The name is a reference to Austrian-born actor and US politician Arnold Schwarzenegger, who is widely known as The Terminator, a character he plays in the movies.)

During the 1998 Olympics in Nagano, Japan, Maier had one of the most dramatic crashes in televised skiing history when he lost control during a downhill run. He went flying 30 feet (9 m) in the air, landed on his helmet, and rammed through two safety fences at an estimated 80 miles (129 km) per hour. To everyone's amazement, Maier stood up and walked away from the crash. Several days later, he won gold medals in the giant slalom and super-G events.

He is also remembered for an even more astonishing comeback following a near-fatal motorcycle accident in 2001, in which he nearly lost a leg. After extensive surgery and rehabilitation, he went on to win a silver medal in 2006 Olympic Games in Turin, Italy.

Maier retired from the sport in 2009 but is still a celebrity in Austria and the world of downhill skiing.

THE LIPIZZANER HORSES

The Spanish Riding School was founded in the sixteenth century to provide horses for the royal Hapsburg family. Today, performances by the Spanish Riding School are one of Vienna's most popular attractions. The professional riders enter the school as apprentices as young as seventeen and spend five years learning how to train horses and at least another ten years perfecting the art of riding. During performances, the riders wear brown uniforms with gold buttons and black hats with gold braiding.

The well-trained white horses at Austria's Spanish Riding School literally dance for their audiences. They pirouette and do the capriole, that is, leap with all four legs off the ground and kick the hind legs out before landing back on the same spot.

The high-stepping horses are known as Lipizzaners. This breed gets its name from Lipizza, a place near Trieste, formerly a part of the Austro-Hungarian Empire, where the stud producing these horses was located in the early twentieth century. The horses are of Spanish, Arabian, and Berber ancestry. They are raised and receive their first training in the small town of Piber, Styria, before being sent to Vienna.

The famous horses of the riding school in Vienna perform in the beautiful baroque riding hall, which was built by Fischer von Erlach in 1735. The riding hall was used as a ballroom during the Congress of Vienna (the epic conference in 1814 at which the great nations tried to reconstitute Europe after Napoleon's defeat).

Money earned from performances at the riding school is used to buy food, uniforms, and boots. The school is economically viable because the Viennese are willing to pay to watch the horses and riders perform. Traditionally, only men rode the Lipizzaner horses, but in 2008, two young women, an Austrian and a Briton, passed the entrance exam and were accepted for training—the first women riders in 436 years. Today, the school, which celebrated its 450th anniversary in 2015, turns out the most famous classical-style equestrian performers in the world.

OTHER SPORTS

Austria's Alpine terrain has given rise to leisure pursuits other than skiing and mountaineering. Hang gliding and ballooning are more recent entrants on the scene. Austrians and tourists alike enjoy the thrill of parapente gliding—flying down a mountain slope in tandem with an experienced instructor by parapente, a steerable parachute. Professional Alpine climbers use the parapente as a speedy way to return home after reaching the peak.

Cycling has always been popular with vacationers in Austria, and it is common to find bicycles for rent at train stations. Specialist mountain bicycles are also available for hire, making a cycle tour of the Alps easily accessible. In the summer lakes attract water-skiers, fishing fans, and swimmers.

Apart from the more active sports, many Austrians visit health spas in various parts of the country. Some of Austria's spas are centuries old and have acquired a reputation for curing or alleviating particular medical problems.

Parapente, or paragliding, in the Alps is a popular leisure activity among courageous types.

INTERNET LINKS

www.austria.info/us
This Austrian tourism site offers information on various sporting, cultural, and family activities.

www.srs.at/en_US/start-en
This home site of the Spanish riding School in Vienna has photos and articles.

FESTIVALS

A young woman wears traditional clothing at the
Villacher Kirchtag folk festival.

12

I N AUSTRIA, THERE ARE PLENTY of good reasons for merriment and remembrance. The Austrian calendar year is marked with religious and state holidays, arts and music festivals, and seasonal agricultural celebrations.

The roots of some traditions go back to ancient times, and others to the Middle Ages—for example, the *Kranzelreiten* festival harkens back to medieval days when the plague might leave only one marriageable girl in a village and perhaps three male survivors to contend for her hand.

The Christmas carol "Silent Night," heard throughout the Christian world at Christmastime, was written by Austrian Franz Gruber. It was first performed on Christmas Eve in 1818 in the village of Oberndorf. As the story goes, this carol was accompanied by guitars because mice had gnawed away at the organ's bellows.

A festive parade features a traditional beer wagon being pulled by a team of horses.

Conductor Zubin Mehta leads the Vienna Philharmonic Orchestra at the 2015 New Year's performance at the Musikverein concert hall in Vienna.

Today, this festival features a joust where men on horseback try to spear a ring. The reward for the winner is a *kranzel* (KRAHNT-zel), or wreath. Other special days are more recent, such as National Day on October 26, which commemorates independence and the Declaration of Neutrality in 1955.

WINTER FUN

Many people worldwide regard Vienna as the penultimate place to celebrate the New Year. Throughout Austria, New Year's Eve and Day are marked with parties and fabulous fancy-dress balls, but Vienna holds the most elegant, most renowned festivities of all. People flock to Vienna for its luxurious events. The New Year's Eve Ball at the Hofburg Vienna (the Imperial Palace) is probably the world's most lavish formal affair. Tickets are said to be nearly impossible to obtain, however, so luckily there are other galas held at City Hall and the city's leading hotels. Strains of Johann Strauss' "Blue Danube Waltz" are a must for the evening's musical theme. The Vienna Philharmonic presents an annual New Year's Day concert, filled with Strauss waltzes, of course; and the Vienna State Opera presents its traditional performance of Johann Strauss's *Die Fledermaus*. The events are televised for those folks not lucky enough to be there.

New Year's Day also kicks off *Fasching*, or Carnival, which lasts until Lent. Things really get going in February, when parades are held in towns and villages, with dancers wearing masks, hats, and elaborate costumes. The most famous Fasching festivals are in Tyrol and the Salzkammergut region.

SPRING CELEBRATIONS

EASTER This day is a major Christian festival in Austria, as it is throughout the Christian world. It falls on the Sunday after the first full moon in spring and is preceded by Lent, forty days of fasting and abstinence. As the last week of Lent ends, a service is held on Good Friday to recall Jesus Christ's death on the cross for the sins of the world. Easter Sunday celebrates the resurrection of Christ with singing, processions, and music from church bells, choirs, and village bands.

Easter eggs are for sale at a street market in Salzburg.

The Easter Rabbit brings Easter eggs to children in a modern expression of an old fertility rite (both the egg and the rabbit symbolize fertility). The rabbit was the escort of the Germanic goddess Ostara, who gives her name to the festival.

Less common is the ritual *schmeckostern* (SHMECK-os-tern), or "Easter smacks." On Easter Monday and Tuesday, men and women in parts of Austria and Germany "beat" each other with birch, cherry, or vine branches in the belief that these ritual beatings bring good luck, long life, and prosperity.

CORPUS CHRISTI This religious holiday is celebrated in May each year throughout Austria. It falls on the Thursday after Holy Trinity Sunday, which follows the fiftieth day after Easter Sunday. Colorful processions and parades take place in towns and villages across Austria, some on lakes in the Salzkammergut region. In some places, Corpus Christi is an occasion to put on traditional clothes.

SUMMERTIME

Midsummer celebrations (which are actually the beginning of summer) in Austria have a pagan origin, but the event is kept alive by rural Roman Catholics. Around June 21 each year, towns and villages all over Austria commemorate the longest day of the year with bonfires, music, and parties.

THE SALZBERG FESTIVAL Every summer, Austria hosts a variety of music festivals, but the Salzburg Festival is the most famous and prestigious of them all. Max Reinhardt, the founder of the festival, was the original producer of Hofmannsthal's *Jedermann*, a version of the medieval *Everyman* morality play that is now a trademark of the festival. Any orchestra or opera singer invited to the festival sees such an invitation as a mark of international recognition. Salzburg was the home of Wolfgang Amadeus Mozart, so it is no surprise that his music is always the centerpiece of this annual festival.

Founded in 1920, the Salzburg Festival is now a fine arts gala with theater and opera, concerts and serenades, chamber music and live street theater, and recitals and lectures. It attracts some 250,000 visitors every year, from both home and abroad.

ALMABTRIEB In September, villages throughout the Alps welcome cowherds and their cattle as they return at summer's end from pastures higher up in the mountains. The cowherds decorate their cattle with headdresses of flowers and ribbons and make a long journey with the herds down the Alps in thanksgiving for a safe summer in the mountains. (In old times ,the herds were covered to protect them from demons on the journey.) The cow trains are celebrated with music and dance events, and in some places, they have become major tourist attractions.

AUTUMN DAYS

ALL SOULS' DAY This day, November 2, is another event in the religious calendar when small villages come alive with a procession led by the village band, whose members wear tall white feathers in their caps. The priest often has a loudspeaker to lead the prayers and chants as the villagers walk to the village cemetery. Candles flicker by the graves that are surrounded by flowers placed there by relatives of the dead. Especially on All Souls' Day, Roman Catholics pray for the faithful departed, those believed to be in purgatory because they have died with lesser sins on their souls.

ST. MARTIN'S DAY is celebrated throughout Austria and much of Europe on his feast day, November 11. Martin, who shared his cloak with a poor man, is the patron saint of Austria's easternmost province, Burgenland. Children hold lantern parades through town and everyone enjoys a special feast of roast goose, *Martinigansl* (MAR-tee-nee-GAHN-sel), and red cabbage.

Cows are adorned with flowers, ribbons, and giant bells for this alpine end-of-summer tradition.

BEWARE THE KRAMPUS

The night before St. Nicholas Day is Krampusnacht *(Krampus Night). While children eagerly await the arrival of Saint Nicholas, they also cower in fear at the threat of Krampus. This nightmarish creature is a devilish pre-Christian figure of Germanic folklore that is especially popular in the Alpine regions of Europe. He is often pictured as a furry beast with a long red tongue, horns, a tail, one foot, and a hoof. The beast's role is to whip naughty children with branches—or even, parents warn, to throw them in a sack and take them back to his lair.*

The Krampus is a counterpoint to the benevolent and loving Father Christmas, and the entire tradition is all in fun—though some people are trying to discourage the Krampus tradition as being too frightening for children. Grown men, no doubt reliving their own childhood terrors and delights, love to dress as Krampus and appear at Christmas parades and other public events.

CHRISTMAS

The Christmas season begins on St. Nicholas Day, December 6, and ends on Epiphany, January 6. Christians display nativity scenes in their homes, sing carols, often with a harp accompaniment. Festive lights and decorations adorn public places. On St. Nicholas Day, open-air markets sell Christmas decorations and toys. Some of the biggest celebrations are in the town of Christkindl in Styria.

The Christmas Market in Vienna is a festive celebration of the season and a great tourist attraction.

On Christmas Eve, the mood becomes more sacred as churches throughout the country are crowded with people attending midnight Mass. At St. Stephen's Cathedral in Vienna, entrance tickets have to be distributed to deal with the crowd. Christmas Day is usually spent quietly with the family. The next day, St. Stephen's Day, is for visiting friends and relatives. On Epiphany, children go around the neighborhood singing carols and folk songs to mark the journey of the Three Kings.

INTERNET LINKS

www.ajc.com/news/news/world/krampus-story-austrias-terrifying-christmas-tradit/ncFSX
This amusing presentation of the Krampus tradition includes video.

www.hofburgsilvesterball.com
See photos of Vienna's magnificent New Year's Eve ball and read about formal ball dress codes and etiquette.

www.tourmycountry.com/austria/traditionscustoms.htm
Here is a good overview of the Austrian year of festivals, traditions, and events.

FOOD

A strawberry Linzertorte is a tempting dessert.

13

VIENNA HAS BEEN THE CAPITAL OF Austria for more than a thousand years, which has given it plenty of time to develop a distinctive cuisine. Viennese cuisine is often thought to exemplify the best of Austrian cooking. Some of its most characteristic dishes, such as *Wiener Schnitzel* (veal cutlets) and *Apfelstrudel* (apple strudel) are popular worldwide. However, Austria's regions have their own interesting and delicious variations, reflecting the influences of Italian, Hungarian, Czech, and Bohemian (German) cooking.

MEALTIMES

For breakfast, Austrians have rolls and coffee, followed by *gabelfrühsttück* (GAH-bel-FROOH-shtook), literally a "fork breakfast," a heavier mid-morning meal resembling an American breakfast.

Lunch is the main meal of the day. It is served at noon and usually consists of soup, meat, and vegetables. Supper in the evening is lighter. Austrians take a coffee break, or *jause* (YOW-seh), at around 3 p.m. to enjoy cakes and other pastries.

The Linzertorte, one of Austria's best-known desserts, is said to be the oldest cake in the world. It's a cake made of a ground hazelnut pastry covered with a thick layer of jam and covered with a lattice of pastry strips. The oldest known recipe for this cake dates from 1653.

WHERE TO EAT

Würzelstand (VOOR-zel-shtand), or sausage stands, are the nearest thing in Austria to hot dog stands in the United States. Austrians eat sausages with sauerkraut and dumplings, then wash it all down with a beer. Office workers eat at snack bars called *imbisstube* (IM-bis-shtoo-beh) or casual restaurants called *gasthäuser* (GAHST-HOW-seh). Or they may decide to spend a little more at a wine cellar or wine garden—both are still less formal and costly than hotel restaurants—that serves snacks, buffet lunches, and dinners. The wine cellars started out only serving wine, but they are now visited more for the food.

Austrian dining etiquette often appears formal to outsiders. Where North Americans would comfortably use their hands when eating a sandwich, Austrians use a knife and fork. Expensive restaurants often expect their customers to wear a tie and jacket, and in Vienna, even moderately priced restaurants prefer diners to wear formal dress. The general rule to outsiders is: when in doubt, dress up.

PASTRIES AND DESSERTS

The Austrians' love of food is best represented by the tempting array of pastries found in the *konditorei* (kon-dee-toh-RAY), or pastry shop. Pastries and desserts are collectively called *mehlspeisen* (mehl-SCHPY-sehn) in Austria. Famous Austrian pastries and desserts include a rich chocolate cake called *sachertorte* (SAH-kher-TOR-teh), a sponge cake called *gugelhupf* (KOOH-gehl-hoopf), chocolate hazelnut pudding, pancakes called *palatschinken* (pah-lah-SHING-kehn) stuffed with meat or a sweet filling, a

Customers line up at a Wurstelbox food stand in a Vienna park.

sweet called *zwetschkenknödel* (SZWETCH-ken-KNOO-del) made of damson plums (sugar lumps replace the pits and the fruit is wrapped in a dumpling), *kaiserschmarren* (KAI-ser-SHMAH-rehn), or "emperor's omelette," and pancakes cut in pieces and mixed with jam or fruit and dusted with sugar.

VIENNESE COFFEE

Coffee was introduced in Austria more than four hundred years ago by the Turks. At that time, coffee was not yet known in Europe. Like tea to the British, coffee became an important beverage to Austrians.

Over the past four centuries, the Viennese have transformed coffee drinking into a fine art. They have created more than twenty varieties of coffee, including *mokka* (MOK-kah), a small cup of thick black coffee; *kleiner brauner* (klai-ner BROW-ner), a small cup of coffee with a dash of milk; *grosser brauner* (groh-ser BROW-ner), a large cup of coffee with a dash of milk; *melange* (meh-LAHNGE), a half-coffee, half-milk mix with a frothy crown; *kaffee mit schlag* (kah-FAY mit shlahg), coffee with milk and whipped cream; *doppelschlag* (DOP-pel-shlahg), coffee with a double portion of whipped cream; *einspänner* (AIN-shpan-ner), literally a "one-horse coach," actually a glass of coffee topped with whipped cream; *Türkischer* (TOOR-kish-er), black coffee boiled in a copper pot and served in tiny cups, and *kapuziner* (kah-poo-ZI-ner), a little coffee with a lot of milk.

There are many other coffee varieties, but one thing is always the same—Viennese coffee does not come without a glass of water piped in from the Alps. Some people say that this tradition is part of Austrian hospitality; others give a practical reason—to get rid of the powerful after-taste of the coffee with a sip of water.

Viennese coffee topped with whipped cream is an elegant treat.

REGIONAL FOOD

A favorite hot dish in the Alpine regions, especially among skiers just in from the cold outdoors, is a bowl of *leberknödelsuppe* (LAY-ber-KNOO-del-soop-eh), soup with beef- or pork-liver dumplings, or a plate of *speck* (shpeck), smoked bacon.

Goulash, commonly eaten in Austria as a whole meal in itself, includes green peppers, tomatoes, onions, beef or pork, and paprika. Contrary to what many people think, goulash does not contain sour cream.

Noodles are a Carinthian specialty. They may be stuffed with cheese, meat, or fruit. Styria is well known for its *sterz* (stertz), or mashes made from flour. *Türkensterz* (TOER-kehn-stertz) is a corn mash served with soup. Another Styrian specialty is *würzelfleisch* (VOORT-zel-fly-sh), a pork stew with vegetables.

Fondue, a Swiss dish of melted cheese, is another favorite in Austria. White wine is heated in a casserole rubbed with garlic. Grated cheese is added, with cornstarch and a dash of nutmeg. Fondue is eaten communally, straight from the pot. Diners spear cubes of crusty bread on skewers and dip the bread into the hot cheese mixture.

THE IMPORTANCE OF FOOD

In Tyrol, the importance of food is reflected in folktales and festivals. This may have to do with the fact that food was difficult to find during winter and survival depended entirely on the family's store of food from the summer and fall.

Winters were harsh in the mountainous regions and being prepared for the worst meant smoking or salting food and stacking firewood ready for use. Wasting food was unforgivable. The Tyrolean folktale character Frau Hütt was turned into stone because she wasted food.

The importance of food is also seen in the way All Souls' Day is still sometimes observed in Tyrol. All Souls' Day commemorates the souls of the dead and the belief that souls not yet purified for heaven may be helped by prayer. In parts of Tyrol and northern Italy, this is linked to a belief that the dead may return on All Souls' Day. So strong is the belief that food is left overnight on the kitchen table for returning souls.

INTERNET LINKS

www.food.com/topic/austrian
Food.com offers Austrian recipes using US measurements.

www.tasteofaustria.org
The Austrian Embassy in the United States presents this excellent culinary site which goes well beyond recipes.

www.tourmycountry.com/austria/dining.htm
This site offers an in-depth look at Austrian cuisine, including regional dishes and historical notes.

WIENER SCHNITZEL (VEAL CUTLETS)

In Vienna, veal is the traditional meat for this dish, but it can also be made with pork, using pork tenderloin cutlets.

1 cup (120 grams) all-purpose flour
3 teaspoons (17.06 g) kosher salt, divided
2 large eggs
2 tablespoons (30 g) heavy cream
pinch nutmeg
2 cups (300 g) fine plain dried breadcrumbs
½ pound (230 g) veal scaloppine (cutlets)
Freshly ground black pepper
2 cups (475 milliliters) vegetable oil or lard
(lard is traditional)
3 tablespoons (42.5 g) unsalted butter
1 lemon, cut into 4 wedges

Line a large baking sheet with a double layer of paper towels. Set out three large, shallow bowls. In one bowl, whisk flour with 1 teaspoon (8 g) salt. In another bowl, lightly whisk eggs, cream, and nutmeg. In the third bowl, mix breadcrumbs with 2 teaspoons salt. Pound veal slices between sheets of plastic wrap to ⅛ inch (3 mL) thickness, being careful not to tear. Season meat lightly with salt and pepper.

In a large skillet, heat oil over medium heat to 350˚F (175˚C), using a deep-fry thermometer to measure temperature. Add butter to skillet and adjust heat to maintain temperature.

Dredge 2 veal slices in flour mixture; shake off excess. Dip in egg. Turn to coat; shake off excess. Dredge in breadcrumbs, pressing to adhere; shake off excess. Transfer slices to skillet. Using a large spoon, carefully baste the top of the veal with the hot oil. Cook until breading puffs and starts to brown, about 1 minute. Turn and cook until browned, about 1 minute longer. Transfer to paper towel-lined sheet. Repeat with remaining veal slices.

Serve with spätzle, noodles, or potato salad. Garnish with lemon wedges and parsley.

WIENER APFELSTRUDEL (VIENNESE APPLE STRUDEL)

This pastry roll-up is one of Austria's most iconic desserts.

¼ cup (40 grams) raisins (purple or golden)
3 tablespoons dark rum (or orange juice), warmed
½ cup (100 g) plus 1 tablespoon sugar
1 ¼ teaspoons (3.25 g) ground cinnamon
½ teaspoon (4 g) coarse salt
3 tart apples, such as Granny Smith, peeled, cored, and thinly sliced
1 tablespoon (½ lemon) fresh lemon juice

½ cup (75 g) dried fine breadcrumbs
6 sheets phyllo dough, roughly 13 by 16 inches (33 by 40 cm), thawed if frozen
1 stick (115 g) unsalted butter, melted
Lightly sweetened whipped cream, for serving

Preheat oven to 375˚F (190˚C). Soak raisins in warm rum or juice; set aside. Prepare apple slices and toss with lemon juice. Combine sugar, cinnamon, and salt in a large bowl; set aside 3 tablespoons of the mixture. Drain raisins. Stir apples into sugar mixture, and add raisins and breadcrumbs.

Brush 1 sheet phyllo with butter, and sprinkle with 1 teaspoon reserved sugar mixture. Top with remaining 5 sheets phyllo, layering with butter and sugar mixture. Scatter filling on phyllo, leaving a ½-inch border. Starting with a long end, roll up to enclose filling. Place strudel, seam side down, on a parchment-lined baking sheet. Brush top with remaining butter; sprinkle with remaining sugar. Bake until golden brown and cooked through, 45 to 50 minutes. Let cool on a wire rack 10 minutes. Cut into slices. Serve warm with whipped cream.

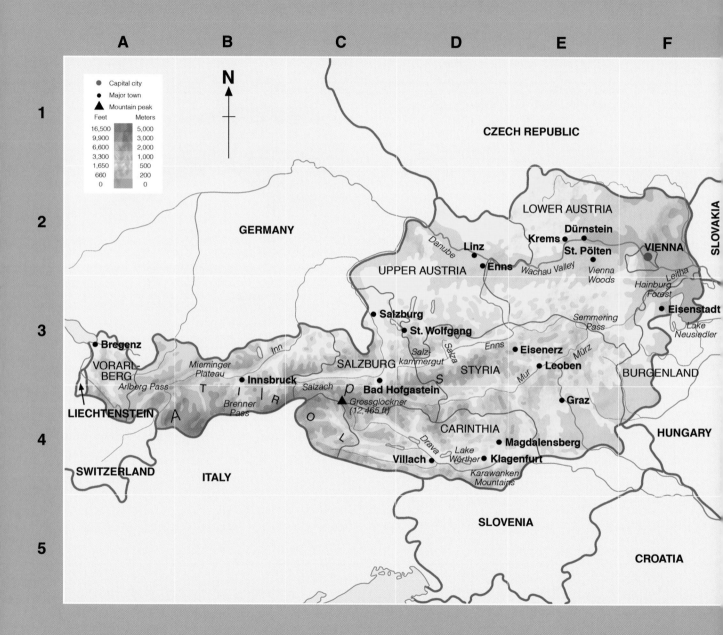

MAP OF AUSTRIA

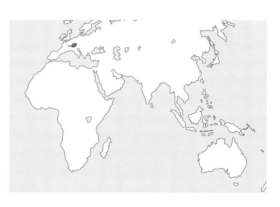

133

ECONOMIC AUSTRIA

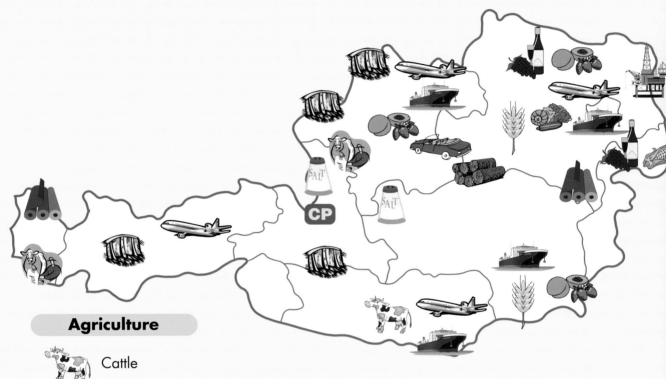

Agriculture

 Cattle

 Corn

 Dairy Products

 Fruit

 Vegetables

 Wheat

Wine

Natural Resources

CP Copper

 Hydroelectricity

Oil

Salt

Timber

Manufacturing

Textiles

Vehicles

Services

 Airport

 Port

ABOUT THE ECONOMY

GROSS DOMESTIC PRODUCT (GDP)
$437.1 billion (2014)

GDP SECTORS
Agriculture 1.3 percent, industry 28.4 percent, services 70.2 percent (2014)

LAND AREA
32,383 square miles (83,871 sq km)

LAND USE
Arable land 16.5 percent, cultivated land 0.8 percent, pastures 21 percent, forests and woodland 47 percent, other 14.4 percent (2011)

AGRICULTURAL PRODUCTS
Grain, potatoes, sugar beets, wine, fruit, dairy products, cattle, poultry, lumber

INDUSTRIES
construction, machinery, vehicles and parts, food, metals, chemicals, lumber and wood, paper and paperboard, communications equipment, tourism

CURRENCY
The euro (EUR) replaced the Austrian Schilling (ATS) in 2002 at a fixed rate of 13.7603 Austrian Schillings per euro.
1 euro = 100 cents
USD 1 = EUR 0.88 (October 2015)
Notes: 5, 10, 20, 50, 100, 200, 500 euros

Coins: 1, 2, 5, 10, 20, 50 cents; 1, 2 euros

LABOR FORCE
3.86 million (2014)

UNEMPLOYMENT RATE
5.6 percent (2014)

POPULATION BELOW POVERTY LINE
4.2 percent (2013)

INFLATION RATE
1.6 percent (2014)

MAJOR TRADE PARTNERS
Germany, Italy, Switzerland, France, the United States, Slovakia, Czech Republic, Netherlands

MAJOR EXPORTS
Machinery and equipment, motor vehicles and parts, paper and paperboard, metal goods, chemicals, iron and steel, textiles, food products

MAJOR IMPORTS
Machinery and equipment, motor vehicles, chemicals, metal goods, oil and oil products, food products

PORTS AND HARBORS (RIVER)
Enns, Krems, Linz, Vienna

AIRPORTS
52 total; 24 with paved runways (2013)

CULTURAL AUSTRIA

Skiers' paradise
Serious skiers are particularly attracted to St. Anton in the Arlberg for its challenging trails. Slopes fall in all directions, and the longest run stretches 5 miles (8 km) from Valluga to St. Anton. The resort also offers friendly trails for families and older skiers. The crowds usually come in late November through Easter.

Eisriesenwelt ice caves
First discovered in 1879, this system of underground caverns near Werfen is characterized by frozen waterfalls and other ice formations. Visitors can join a 75-minute lamp-lit guided tour through the world's largest ice caves between May and October.

Hohensalzburg Castle
Europe's largest fortification stands 94 feet (120 m) above the city of Salzburg. The castle served as a residence for archbishops during the fifteenth and sixteenth centuries. Today, artists come here from around the world to attend courses held by the International Summer Academy of Fine Arts.

Stone Age discovery
In 1908 the Venus of Willendorf, a 4.4-inch (11.2 cm) limestone statuette, was discovered near the town of Willendorf in the Wachau Valley. Believed to be around 26,000 years old, this icon of prehistoric art now sits in the Naturhistorisches Museum in Vienna.

Hofburg Palace
Built between the thirteenth and twentieth centuries, the palace was the residence of the Hapsburg monarchy until 1918. Today, it is the seat of the presidency and an international convention center. It also houses historical and cultural collections and the National Library.

Hofkirche monastery
This Franciscan monastery in Innsbruck houses the tomb of Emperor Maximilian I (1458–1519), where twenty-eight bronze statues representing his ancestors and marble reliefs show scenes from his life. Next to the Hofkirche is the Tyrolean Regional Heritage Museum.

Hohe Tauern National Park
This protected area spreads into the Carinithia, Salzburg, and Tyrol provinces. Here stands Austria's highest mountain, Grossglockner. The country's first national park was established in 1981 and gained international status in 2001.

Graz old town
The capital of Styria was declared a UNESCO World Heritage Site in 1993. Visitors can take a tram up the 1,552-foot (473 m) Schlossberg hill. Here stands Graz's landmark clock tower, which unlike other clocks, tells the hour by its long hand and the minutes by its short hand.

Semmering Railway
Built in the mid-1800s, the Semmering Railway has been named a UNESCO World Heritage Site in recognition of the quality of its tunnels and viaducts, which are still in use today. Passengers can board the train at Vienna and enjoy a scenic mountain ride to Graz.

Haydn Music Festival
During this internationally renowned annual festival in September, classical music lovers get to enjoy Joseph Haydn's music in a historic environment. Many landmarks in Burgenland's capital are linked to Haydn, such as the house where he lived, now a museum.

ABOUT THE CULTURE

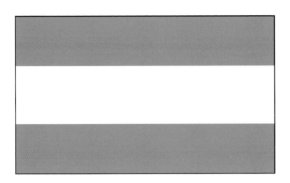

OFFICIAL NAME
Republic of Austria

NATIONAL FLAG
Three horizontal bands, white in the middle sandwiched by red at the top and bottom

NATIONAL ANTHEM
"Österreichische Bundeshymne." Text by Paula von Preradovic, melody from a masonic cantata by Mozart.

CAPITAL
Vienna

OTHER MAJOR CITIES
Graz, Innsbruck, Linz, Salzburg

POPULATION
8,665,550 (2015)

ETHNIC GROUPS
Austrians 91.1 percent, former Yugoslavs 4 percent (includes Croatians, Slovenes, Serbs, and Bosniaks), Turks 1.6 percent, German 0.9 percent, other or unspecified 2.4 percent (2001 census)

RELIGIOUS GROUPS
Roman Catholic 64.1 percent; Protestant, 3.8 percent, Muslim, 7 percent, none or other, 22 percent, unspecified, 2 percent (various sources, 2011)

OFFICIAL LANGUAGE
German

LIFE EXPECTANCY AT BIRTH
total population: 81.39 years
male: 78.76 years
female: 84.15 years (2015)

INTERNET USERS
7.2 million, or 83.7 percent of population (2014)

IMPORTANT ANNIVERSARIES
National Day (October 26), May Day (May 1)

LEADERS IN POLITICS
Heinz Fischer—president since 2004
Werner Faymann—chancellor since 2008

FAMOUS MUSICIANS
Anton Bruckner, Franz Joseph Haydn, Herbert von Karajan, Wolfgang Amadeus Mozart, Arnold Schönberg, Franz Schubert, and Johann Strauss Sr. and Johann Strauss Jr.

OTHER FAMOUS AUSTRIANS
Sigmund Freud (psychologist), Oskar Kokoschka (painter), Andreas Nikolaus Lauda (car racer), Robert Musil (writer), Arnold Schwarzenegger (movie star and US politician), Ludwig Wittgenstein (philosopher)

TIMELINE

IN AUSTRIA	IN THE WORLD
10,000 BCE End of Ice Age in central Europe.	**753 BCE** Rome is founded.
450 BCE Celtic tribes enter Austria.	**116–117 BCE** The Roman Empire reaches its greatest extent, under Emperor Trajan.
30 BCE The Roman Empire expands into Austria.	
400s CE Romans withdraw. Germanic tribes and Slavs occupy Austria.	**600 CE** Height of Mayan civilization.
788 CE Austria becomes part of Charlemagne's empire.	
955 CE Austria becomes an independent state.	**1000** The Chinese perfect gunpowder and begin to use it in warfare.
1278 Hapsburg Dynasty begins.	**1530** Beginning of trans-Atlantic slave trade organized by the Portuguese in Africa.
	1558–1603 Reign of Elizabeth I of England.
1618 Hapsburgs rule Austria and a large part of Europe.	**1620** Pilgrim Fathers sail the *Mayflower* to America.
1683 Ottoman Turks attempt unsuccessfully to capture Vienna.	**1776** US Declaration of Independence.
	1789–1799 French Revolution.
	1861 US Civil War begins.
	1869 The Suez Canal is opened.
	1914 World War I begins.
1918 Austria fights in World War I. Hapsburg Dynasty ends. Austria becomes an independent republic.	
1938 Nazi Germany invades Austria.	

IN AUSTRIA	IN THE WORLD
1939 Austria fights as part of Germany in World War II.	**1939** World War II begins.
1945 Allied forces (United States, Britain, France, Soviet Union) occupy Austria.	**1945** World War II ends.
1955 Allied forces withdraw; Austria becomes independent.	**1949** North Atlantic Treaty Organization (NATO) is formed. **1957** Russians launch *Sputnik 1*. **1966–1969** Chinese Cultural Revolution.
1985 Jörg Haider, leader of the right-wing Freedom Party, wins 10 percent of the vote.	
1986 Controversy over war record of elected president Kurt Waldheim	**1986** Nuclear power disaster at Chernobyl in Ukraine
1989 Hungary begins dismantling its border with Austria.	**1991** Breakup of the Soviet Union
1994–1995 Freedom Party wins 22 percent of the vote. Austria joins the European Union.	
2000 Freedom Party joins coalition government; other EU nations protest.	**2001** World population surpasses six billion.
2004 Heinz Fischer elected president.	
2005 Floods cause devastation as the Danube River bursts its banks.	
2008 Jörg Haider killed in car crash.	**2008** US elects first African American president, Barack Obama.
2010 Heinz Fischer re-elected president.	
2015 Austria and neighboring EU countries disagree over how to handle influx of Middle Eastern refugees.	**2015** War and instability in Middle East and Africa cause mass exodus of refugees to Europe.

GLOSSARY

Anschluss (AHN-shloos)
Union of Austria with Germany after the 1938 German invasion.

dirndl (DURN-duhl)
Traditional dress for women consisting of an embroidered blouse, a lace bodice, a full skirt, and an apron.

föhn (foehn)
A warm, dry wind that blows from the south across the mountains in spring and autumn.

gemütlichkeit (geh-MOOT-likh-keit)
A jovial attitude that establishes a warm and friendly atmosphere.

heuriger (HI-ree-geh)
A wine tavern that serves fresh, new wine produced each year.

High German
A division of the German language that originated in the German highlands. High Austrian German is the "official" form in Austria.

jause (YOW-seh)
A mid-afternoon coffee break.

konditorei (kon-dee-toh-RAY)
A pastry shop where customers can sit down to have coffee and pastries or order to take out.

langlauf (LAHNG-lauf)
Cross-country skiing.

lederhosen (LAY-der-HOH-sern)
Traditional dress for men consisting of leather shorts with ornamental suspenders and a belt.

Lipizzaner
A breed of horse developed for the Hapsburg emperors and used today at the Spanish Riding School.

Österreich (OOST-er-rike)
The name for Austria meaning Eastern Kingdom.

sachertorte (SAH-kher-TOR-teh)
A famous Viennese cake filled with apricot jam and iced with chocolate.

schloss (shloss)
A castle or residence of nobility built during the Habsburg era. Many have been converted into hotels.

strudel (SHTROO-duhl)
A light pastry with various fillings.

social partnership
An arrangement where management and trade unions meet to negotiate wages and prices.

waltz
A three-step dance, characterized by formal slow steps or whirling fast steps.

wiener schnitzel (VEE-ner SHNIT-zuhl)
A fried, breaded veal cutlet.

FOR FURTHER INFORMATION

BOOKS

Beller, Steven. *A Concise History of Austria*. New York: Cambridge University Press, 2011.

DK Publishing. *DK Eyewitness Travel Guide: Austria*. New York: DK Publishing, 2014.

Gieler, Peter. *Austria—Culture Smart!: A quick guide to customs and etiquette*. London: Kuperard, 2007.

Pataki, Allison. *The Accidental Empress: A Novel*. New York: Howard Books, 2015.

Trapp, Maria Augusta. *The Story of the Trapp Family Singers*. New York: HarperCollins Publishers, originally published 1949; reissue 2001.

WEBSITES

Austrian Embassy, Washington, DC. www.austria.org

Austrian National Tourist Office. www.austria.info/us

Central Intelligence Agency World Factbook: Austria. www.cia.gov/library/publications/the-world-factbook/geos/au.html

European Union: Austria. europa.eu/about-eu/countries/member-countries/austria/index_en.htm

New York Times, The. Times Topics: Austria. topics.nytimes.com/top/news/international/countriesandterritories/austria/index.html

MUSIC

Edelweiss. Vienna Boys' Choir. Cobra Entertainment LLC, 2009.

Music From Old Vienna. Naxos, 1994.

The Sound of Austria: A Treasury of Alpine Folk Music. Dorian Recordings, 1994.

DVDS/FILMS

The Best of Austria. TravelVideoStore.com, 2006.

The Children Who Cheated the Nazis. FilmRise, 2000.

The Sound of Music. Twentieth Century Fox, 1965.

BIBLIOGRAPHY

Bischof, Gunter and Anton Pelinka. *Austrian Historical Memory and National Identity*. New Brunswick, NJ: Transaction Publishers, 1997.

Central Intelligence Agency, The World Factbook. http://www.cia.gov/library/publications/the-world-factbook/geos/au.html .

EurActiv.com. "Xenophobia on the increase in Austria." October 13, 2015. http://www.euractiv.com/sections/justice-home-affairs/xenophobia-increase-austria-318458.

Kandell, Jonathan. "Kurt Waldheim dies at 88; ex-UN chief hid Nazi past." *The New York Times*, June 14, 2007. http://www.nytimes.com/2007/06/14/world/europe/14iht-waldheim.3.6141106.html?_r=0.

Kern, Soeren. "Austria: Muslims Outnumber Catholics in Vienna Schools." Gatestone Institute, March 26, 2014. http://www.gatestoneinstitute.org/4229/austria-muslims-vienna-schools .

Local, The. http://www.thelocal.at .

Marchetti, Silvia. "The South Tyrol identity crisis: to live in Italy, but feel Austrian." *The Guardian*, May 30, 2014. http://www.theguardian.com/education/2014/may/30/south-tyrol-live-in-italy-feel-austrian.

OECD Better Life Index. Austria. http://www.oecdbetterlifeindex.org/countries/austria .

PBS. *How Art Made the World*. http://www.pbs.org/howartmadetheworld/episodes/human/venus.

Republik Osterreich Parliament. http://www.parlament.gv.at/ENGL/index.shtml.

Rose, Phil Fox. "Fr. Helmut Schüller's "Catholic Tipping Point" Tour Calls for Disobedience." *Patheos*, July 19, 2013. http://www.patheos.com/blogs/philfoxrose/2013/07/fr-helmut-schullers-catholic-tipping-point-tour-calls-for-disobedience.

United States Holocaust Memorial Museum. http://www.ushmm.org/wlc/en/article.php?ModuleId=10005452.

Visual Arts Encyclopedia. http://www.visual-arts-cork.com/prehistoric/venus-of-willendorf.htm.

Wooden, Cindy. "Pope tells Austrian bishops to respond to crisis by being missionaries." Catholic News Service, CNS News, Jan. 31, 2014. http://www.catholicnews.com/services/englishnews/2014/pope-tells-austrian-bishops-to-respond-to-crisis-by-being-missionaries.cfm.

INDEX

INDEX